This is the day
which the LORD
hath made . . .

and be glad in it.

P S A L M 118:24

REMEMBER THIS . . .
Many seek Him . . .
Who has loved them . . .
through you.

REVEREND RICHARD M. FREEMAN

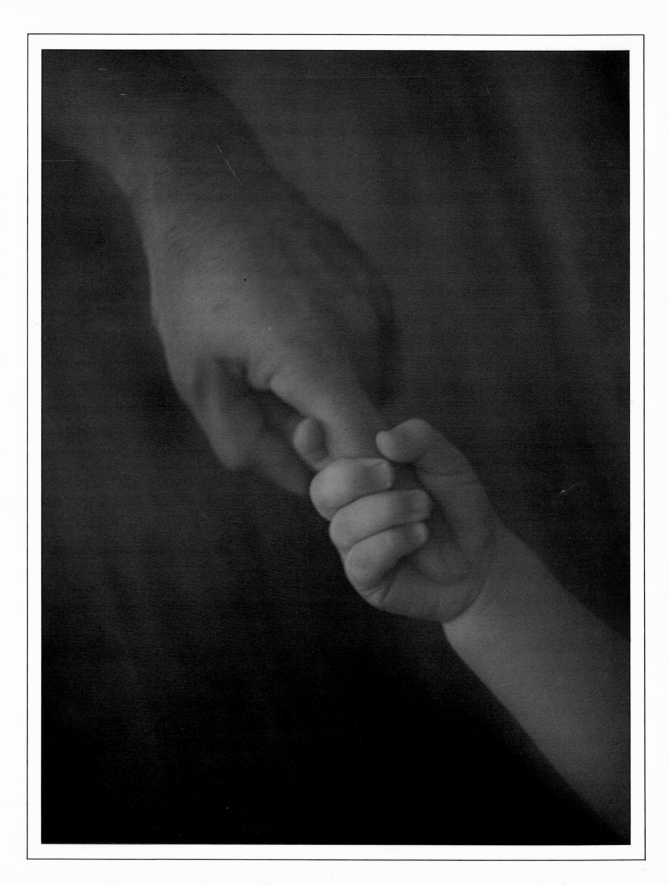

This is the day
which the LORD
hath made . . .

Rejoice

and be glad in it.

P S A L M 118:24

With beautiful thoughts and inspiring prayers by
Peter Marshall, Anne Ortlund, Billy Graham,
Marjorie Holmes, Robert Schuller, Joni Eareckson,
Keith Miller, Catherine Marshall, Ralph Carmichael,
Ruth Bell Graham, Wilferd A. Peterson, Ann Kiemel,
Norman Vincent Peale, Evie, Lloyd John Ogilvie,
Helen Keller, Kurt Kaiser, Anne Murchison,
Ray C. Stedman, Helen Steiner Rice,
and many more contributors offering
messages of love, praise and reassurance.

EDITED AND DESIGNED

BY

RONALD E. GARMAN

WORD BOOKS
PUBLISHER
WACO, TEXAS

ACKNOWLEDGMENTS

The publisher and editor express their appreciation to all those who generously gave permission to reprint copyrighted material. Diligent effort has been made to identify, locate, contact and secure permission to use copyrighted material. If any permissions or acknowledgments have been inadvertently omitted or if such permissions were not received by the time of publication, the publisher would sincerely appreciate receiving complete information so that correct credit can be given in future editions.

"THE STUDY OF GOD'S WORD" by J. W. ALEXANDER, from *Leaves of Gold.* Copyright © 1948 by A. C. and D. G. Remley. Revised Edition 1964. Used by permission. "BETWEEN THE HUMBLE" by HOSEA BALLOU. From *Prelude to Prayer (A Pocket Guide to Prayer for Women).* Copyright © 1939, 1959. The Standard Publishing Company, Cincinnati, Ohio, a Division of Standex International Corporation. Used by permission. "GO FORTH NOBLY" by PHILLIP BROOKS. Copyright © 1978 by Al Bryant. Excerpt from December 31, *LoveSongs,* published by WORD BOOKS/Waco, Texas. Used by permission. "FLOWERS FROM PARADISE" by THOMAS BROOKS. From *Prelude to Prayer (A Pocket Guide to Prayer For Women).* Copyright © 1939 (1959). The Standard Publishing Company, Cincinnati, Ohio, Division of Standex International Corporation. Used by permission. "KINDNESS" by AL BRYANT. Copyright © 1978 by Al Bryant. Excerpt from July 6, *LoveSongs.* Published by WORD BOOKS/Waco, Texas. Used by permission. "QUIETNESS" by AL BRYANT. Copyright © 1978 by Al Bryant. Excerpt from April 9, *LoveSongs.* Published by WORD BOOKS/Waco, Texas. Used by permission. "IF YOU ARE LOOKING" by AL BRYANT. Copyright © 1978 by Al Bryant. Excerpt from November 15, *LoveSongs.* Published by WORD BOOKS/Waco, Texas. Used by permission. "WHAT BETTER WAY" by AL BRYANT. Copyright © 1978 by Al Bryant. Excerpt from November 26, *LoveSongs.* Published by WORD BOOKS/ Waco, Texas. Used by permission. "IF A GENEROUS SPIRIT" by AL BRYANT. Copyright © 1978 by Al Bryant. Excerpt from July 21, *LoveSongs.* Published by WORD BOOKS/Waco, Texas. Used by permission. "GOD'S EYES" by AL BRYANT. Copyright © 1978 by Al Bryant. Excerpt from December 29, *LoveSongs.* Published by WORD BOOKS/Waco, Texas. Used by permission. "HE'S EVERYTHING TO ME" by RALPH CARMICHAEL. Copyright © 1964 by Lexicon Music, Inc. ASCAP. All Rights Reserved. International Copyright Secured. Used by Special Permission. "WHEN WE CALL ON GOD" by ELIZABETH CHARLES, from *Prelude to Prayer (A Pocket Guide to Prayer for Women).* Copyright © 1939 (1959), The Standard Publishing Company, Cincinnati, Ohio, Division of Standex International Corporation. Used by permission. "SOMETIME WE'LL UNDERSTAND" by MAXWELL N. CORNELIUS. Copyright © 1970 by WORD BOOKS/Waco, Texas. Excerpt from pages 66-67, *When Sorrow Comes,* by Robert V. Ozment. Used by permission. "LET US GIVE" by A. POWELL DAVIES. Excerpt from "A Minister Says," in the September, 1954 issue of *Childhood Education.* Copyright © 1954 by the Association for Childhood Education International. Reprinted by permission of the Association for Childhood Education International, 3615 Wisconsin Avenue, N.W., Washington, D.C. "IF I CAN STOP ONE HEART FROM BREAKING" by EMILY DICKINSON. From *The Complete Poems of Emily Dickinson,* edited by Thomas H. Johnson. Reprinted with permission of Little Brown and Co., Boston, Massachusetts. "O ETERNAL GOD" by JAMES DOBSON, SR. Copyright © 1980 by James C. Dobson. Excerpt of prayer from page 55, *Straight Talk to Men and Their Wives.* Published by WORD BOOKS/Waco, Texas. Used by permission. "ETERNAL LOVE" by JAMES C. DOBSON, SR. Copyright © 1980 by James C. Dobson. Excerpt from page 15, *Straight Talk to Men and Their Wives.* Published by WORD BOOKS/Waco, Texas. Used by permission. "A WEDDING PRAYER" by JAMES C. DOBSON, SR. Copyright © 1980 by James C. Dobson. Excerpt from pages 55-56, *Straight Talk to Men and Their Wives.* Published by WORD BOOKS/Waco, Texas. Used by permission. "THE GREATEST THING" by HENRY DRUMMOND. Copyright © 1978 by Al Bryant. Excerpt from July 5, *LoveSongs.* Published by WORD BOOKS/Waco, Texas. Used by permission. "I LIFT THE BRANCH" by MICHAEL DUBINA. Copyright © 1980 by Michael Dubina. Used by permission. "A TREASURE FOR THE NEW YEAR" by HENRY VAN DYKE, from *Leaves of Gold.* Copyright © 1948 by A. C. and D. G. Remley. Revised Edition 1964. Used by permission. "HOME" by HENRY VAN DYKE. Excerpt from *Leaves of Gold.* Copyright © 1948 by A. C. and D. G. Remley. Revised Edition 1964. Used by permission. "JOY COMES" by JONI EARECKSON. Copyright © 1981 by Educational Products Division of Word, Inc., Waco, Texas. Excerpt from *Trust and Obey,* 144LL. Used by permission. "I DO NOT MIND" by JONI EARECKSON. Copyright © 1981 by Educational Products Division of Word, Inc., Waco, Texas. Excerpt from *Trust and Obey,* 144LL. Used by permission. "THE ANSWER" by GEORGE L. EHRMAN. Copyright © 1964 by George L. Ehrman. Used by permission. Excerpt from "PRAYER IS LIFE" by JAMES DILLET FREEMAN. Copyright © 1981 by *Daily Word.* Used by permission. "REMEMBER THIS . . ." by REVEREND RICHARD M. FREEMAN. Copyright © 1981 by Reverend Richard M. Freeman. Used by permission. "PRAYER FOR EACH DAY" by REVEREND RICHARD M. FREEMAN. Copyright © 1981 by Reverend Richard M. Freeman. Used by permission. "KEEP THE FIRES BURNING" by REVEREND RICHARD M. FREEMAN. Copyright © 1981 by Reverend Richard M. Freeman. Used by permission. "A GIFT OF THE HEART" by REVEREND RICHARD M. FREEMAN. Copyright © 1981 by Reverend Richard M. Freeman. Used by permission. "YOUR LOVE IS A GRACE FOR ME" by RONALD E. GARMAN. Copyright © 1981 by Ronald E. Garman. Used by permission. "SIMPLE JOYS" by RONALD E. GARMAN. Copyright © 1981 by Ronald E. Garman. Used by permission of author. "CHERISH EACH DAY" by RONALD E. GARMAN. Copyright © 1981 by Ronald E. Garman. Used by permission. "PRAYER" by BILLY GRAHAM. Copyright © 1981 by Billy Graham. Excerpt from page 155, *Till Armageddon,* published by WORD BOOKS/Waco, Texas. Used by permission. "OFF AND ON" by BILLY GRAHAM. Copyright © 1977 by Billy Graham. Excerpt from page 181, *How to Be Born Again,* published by WORD BOOKS/Waco, Texas. Used by permission. "REJOICE" by BILLY GRAHAM. Copyright © 1981 by Billy Graham. Excerpt from page 146, *Till Armageddon.* Published by WORD BOOKS/Waco, Texas. Used by permission. "FORGIVENESS" by BILLY GRAHAM. Copyright © 1977 by Billy Graham. Excerpt from page 128, *How to Be Born Again.* Published by WORD BOOKS/Waco, Texas. Used by permission. "INCREDIBLE" by BILLY GRAHAM. Copyright © 1981 by Billy Graham. Excerpt from page 166, *Till Armageddon.* Published by WORD BOOKS/Waco, Texas. Used by permission. "O GOD" by BILLY GRAHAM. Copyright © 1977 by Billy Graham. Excerpt from page 169, *How to Be Born Again.* Published by WORD BOOKS/Waco, Texas. Used by permission. "UNTIL" by BILLY GRAHAM. Copyright © 1981 by Billy Graham. Excerpt from page 219, *Till Armageddon.* Published by WORD BOOKS/Waco, Texas. Used by permission. "JOY" by BILLY GRAHAM. Copyright © 1981 by Billy Graham. Excerpt from page 38, *Till Armageddon.* Published by WORD BOOKS/Waco, Texas. Used by permission. "THE WORD OF GOD" by BILLY GRAHAM. Copyright © 1977 by Billy Graham. Excerpt from page 45, *How to Be Born Again.* Published by WORD BOOKS/Waco, Texas. Used by permission. "O THOU" by RUTH BELL GRAHAM. Copyright © 1977 by Ruth Bell Graham. Excerpt from page 61, *Sitting by My Laughing Fire.* Published by WORD BOOKS/Waco, Texas. Used by permission. "PRAY" by RUTH BELL GRAHAM. Copyright © 1977 by Ruth Bell Graham. Excerpt from page 47, *Sitting by My Laughing Fire.* Published by WORD BOOKS/ Waco, Texas. Used by permission. "I AM ONLY ONE" by EDWARD EVERETT HALE. From: *Treasury of Religious Verse.* Used by permission of Fleming H. Revell Company. "GOD CONVERSES" by JEANNE HILL. Copyright © 1978 by WORD BOOKS/Waco, Texas. Excerpt from page 95, *Daily Breath.*Used by permission. "THE LESSON OF LOSS"by MARJORIE HOLMES. Excerpt from "The Lesson of Loss" from *I've Got to Talk to Somebody, God* by Marjorie Holmes. Copyright © 1968, 1969 by Marjorie Holmes Mighell. Reprinted by permission of Doubleday and Company, Inc. "THE NEW DIMENSION OF LOVE" by MARJORIE HOLMES. Excerpt from "New Dimensions of Love" from *I've Got to Talk to Somebody, God* by Marjorie Holmes. Copyright © 1968, 1969 by Marjorie Holmes Mighell. Reprinted by permission of Doubleday & Company, Inc. "ALL THESE THINGS" by NAN HOUSTON. Copyright © 1980 by *Daily Word.* Used by permission. "THROUGH JESUS CHRIST" by RUBEN JOB. Copyright © 1976 by WORD BOOKS/Waco, Texas. Excerpt from page 109, *The Gift of Easter* by Floyd Thatcher. Used by permission. "I AM WILLING LORD" by KURT KAISER. Copyright © 1976 by Word Music, (ASCAP), A Division of Word, Inc., Waco, Texas. Used by permission. "PASS IT ON" by KURT KAISER. Copyright © 1969 by Lexicon Music, Inc. ASCAP. All Rights Reserved. International Copyright Secured. Used by Special Permission. "LOOK TO THIS DAY" by KALIDASA, a Sanscrit Proverb from *Golden Treasury of the Familiar* by Ralph L. Woods. Published by Macmillan, 1980. Reprinted by permission of Macmillan Publishing Co., Inc., New York. "RISK EVERYTHING" by EVIE KARLSSON. Copyright © 1978 by Educational Products Division of Word, Inc., Waco, Texas. Excerpt from *Evie,* 111LL. Used by permission. "SMILE THROUGH THE TEARS" by W. PHILLIP KELLER. Copyright © 1981 by W. Phillip Keller. Excerpt from page 112, *Salt for Society.* Published by WORD BOOKS/ Waco, Texas. Used by permission. "GOD MAKES VERY SURE" by W. PHILLIP KELLER. Copyright © 1979 by W. Phillip Keller. Excerpt from page 132, *A Gardener Looks at the Fruit of the Spirit.* Published by WORD BOOKS/Waco, Texas. Used by permission. "GIVE TO THE WORLD" by W. PHILLIP KELLER. Copyright © 1981 by W. Phillip Keller. Excerpt from pages 121-122, *Salt for Society.* Published by WORD BOOKS/Waco, Texas. Used by permission. "I WALK WITH GOD" by W. PHILLIP KELLER. Copyright © 1981 by W. Phillip Keller. Excerpt from page 136, *Salt for Society.* Published by WORD BOOKS/Waco, Texas. Used by permission. "THOSE WHO LIVE" by W. PHILLIP KELLER. Copyright © 1979 by W. Phillip Keller. Excerpt from pages 132-133, *A Gardener Looks at the Fruit of the Spirit.* Published by WORD BOOKS/Waco, Texas. Used by permission. "WITH A GOOD CONSCIENCE" by JOHN F. KENNEDY. From inaugural address, published by Random House, Inc., as *A John F. Kennedy Memorial Miniature.* Copyright © 1966. "ALL THINGS" by CHARLES KINGSLEY. Copyright © 1978 by Al Bryant. Excerpt from February 26, *LoveSongs.* Published by WORD BOOKS/Waco, Texas. Used by permission. "YES, LORD" by ANN KIEMEL. Copyright © 1979 by Educational Products Division of Word, Inc., Waco, Texas. Excerpt from *Yes, Lord!,* 124LL. Used by permission. "I WALKED AWAY" by ANN KIEMEL. Copyright © 1979 by Educational Products Division of Word, Inc., Waco, Texas. Excerpt from *Yes, Lord!,* 124LL. Used by permission. "YOU ARE NEEDED" by ELIZABETH SEARLE LAMB. Copyright © 1981 by *Daily Word.* Used by permission. "A PSALM" by ELINOR LENNEN. Copyright © 1959 by Elinor Lennen. Used by permission. "EACH FAMILY" by L. RICHARD LESSOR. Excerpt from *Married to Merried* by L. Richard Lessor. Copyright © 1972 by Argus Communications, Allen, Texas. Used by permission. Excerpt from "THIS IS GOD'S GOOD DAY" by ROSE ELAINE LIGHTBURNE. Copyright © 1982 by *Daily Word.* Used by permission. "HAND IN HAND" by NADINE BROTHERS LYBARGER. Copyright © 1959 by Nadine Brothers Lybarger. Used by permission. "JESUS' PROMISE" by CATHERINE MARSHALL. Copyright © 1978 by Catherine Marshall. Excerpt from page 31, *The Helper,* published by WORD BOOKS/Waco, Texas. Used with permission. "AS WE BEGIN TO LIVE" by CATHERINE MARSHALL. Copyright © 1978 by Catherine Marshall. Excerpt frnm page 123, *The Helper.* Publisher by WORD BOOKS/Waco, Texas. Used by permission. "I CAN AFFIRM" by CATHERINE MARSHALL. Copyright © 1978 by Catherine Marshall. Excerpt from page 80, *The Helper.* Published by WORD BOOKS/Waco, Texas. Used by permission. "MAY WE" by PETER MARSHALL. Copyright © 1955, 1969 by Catherine Marshall. Used by permission. "O GOD" by PETER MARSHALL. Excerpt from *The Prayers of Peter Marshall.* Copyright © 1949, 1950, 1951, 1954 by Catherine Marshall. Published by Chosen Books, Lincoln, Virginia 22075. Used by permission. "OUR LORD" by PETER MARSHALL. Excerpt from *The Prayers of Peter Marshall.* Copyright © 1949, 1950, 1951, 1954 by Catherine Marshall. Published by Chosen Books, Lincoln, Virginia 22075. Used by permission. "FATHER WE THANK THEE" by PETER MARSHALL. Excerpt from *The Prayers of Peter Marshall.* Copyright © 1949, 1950, 1951, 1954 by Catherine Marshall. Published by Chosen Books, Lincoln, Virginia 22075. Used by permission. "ON THE THRESHOLD OF A NEW YEAR" by PETER MARSHALL. From *The Prayers of Peter Marshall.* Copyright © 1949, 1950, 1951, 1954 by Catherine Marshall. Published by Chosen Books, Lincoln, Virginia 22075. Used by permission. "WHATEVER FORM IT TAKES" by HUGH McLELLAN. From *Prelude to Prayer (A Pocket Guide to Prayer for Women).* Copyright © 1939 (1959). The Standard Publishing Company, Cincinnati, Ohio, Division of Standex International Corporation. Used by permission. "TROUBLE AND PERPLEXITY" by PHILLIP MELANCHTHON. From *Prelude to Prayer (A Pocket Guide to Prayer for Women.)* Copyright © 1939 (1959). The Standard Publishing Company, Cincinnati, Ohio. Used by permission. "SEEK THE GOOD" by J. R. MILLER. Copyright © 1978 by Al Bryant. Excerpt from November 20, *LoveSongs.* Published by WORD BOOKS/Waco, Texas. Used by permission. "I BEGAN TO KEEP A LIST" by KEITH MILLER. Copyright © 1964 by Keith Miller. Excerpt from page 82, *A Taste of New Wine,* published by WORD BOOKS/ Waco, Texas. Used by permission. "RECONNECTION" by KEITH MILLER. Copyright © 1978 by Educational Products Division of Word, Inc., Waco, Texas. Excerpt from *Reconnection,* 113LL. Used by permission. "LIFE BECOMES RICHER" by KEITH MILLER. Copyright © 1964 by Keith Miller. Excerpt from page 81, *A Taste of New Wine.* Published by WORD BOOKS/Waco, Texas. Used by permission. "READING THE SCRIPTURES" by KEITH MILLER. Copyright © 1964 by Keith Miller. Excerpt from page 81, *A Taste of New Wine.* Published by WORD BOOKS/Waco, Texas. Used by permission. "HOW

TODAY IS THE DAY WHICH THE LORD HATH MADE . . . REJOICE AND BE GLAD IN IT

ISBN 0-8499-0311-4 Library of Congress catalog card number: 81-71498

All Scripture quotations are from the King James Version Bible.

WITH SPECIAL APPRECIATION

Although *Rejoice!* has been a labor of love for me, its success is not so much a reflection of my own efforts alone. Rather, it is truly a reflection of the generous and cooperative spirit of the many companies who graciously agreed to grant me permission to reprint copyrighted prose and poetry, and the many authors and artists who were so kind in giving me permission to use their inspired thoughts, writings or prayers. It is also my great fortune to have friends like Merle Oliver and Al Bryant. Merle typed, retyped and continued to type the hundreds of pages of manuscript, letters and special changes, and throughout, she maintained her feminine grace and loveliness of spirit that made my work so easy and wonderful. Al Bryant is Senior Editor at Word, Incorporated, and he is one of the best loved Christian writers and compilers of our time, having more than 50 books to his credit. His advice, counsel and direction were reassuring to me through the many twists and turns on my journey to completing my first book. The selection "True Friendship," facing page to February 25-28, is dedicated to both of them. A very special and heartfelt thank you to my publisher, Floyd Thatcher, Vice-President, Word Books. His personal relationship with Jesus is truly reflected in the kind, honest and caring way he works with those who owe him so very much.   RONALD E. GARMAN

DEDICATION

Dedicated to you, your family
and loved ones . . .
in praise and thanksgiving
to Jesus for the blessings
of my life . . .
especially those blessings
whom I lovingly refer to as
Mother, Mom or Wife.

RONALD E. GARMAN

THIS IS GOD'S GOOD DAY

This is God's good day. It is the day which the Lord has made and I will rejoice and be glad in it.

This day is a new beginning. It is God's gift to me. It offers me another beautiful opportunity to grow and unfold in spiritual consciousness so that I may become more Christlike.

This new day has been bathed in the morning dew and comes to me fresh and clean. This new day is like a clean slate on which I may write another page in my book of life. The nature of the events that will be recorded on this page are determined by my own attitudes of mind and the wisdom and good judgment that I use in directing my thoughts and feelings to make wise choices in the use of my day.

Because I want this day to be gain not loss, to be good not evil, to be success not failure, I will not waste it on trivial things or in shallow thinking. I will not harbor regrets or hurt feelings. I will not allow memories of yesterday's mistakes to cloud my vision, instead I will glean golden memories from the past that help make yesterday's dreams into today's realities.

I look forward with joyous anticipation to this new adventure of God's presence within me that heals, renews, restores, and sustains me in health and wholeness. I will use my thoughts and my physical and emotional energies constructively and creatively to weave love, beauty, peace, poise, harmony, and serenity into the fabric of my life.

This is God's good day. It is the day which the Lord has made and I will rejoice and be glad in it. Today I will pray a little, I will work a little, I will play a little, I will sing a little, I will laugh a little. I will live this day to the glory of God.

ROSE ELAINE LIGHTBURNE

PRAYER IS LIFE

Prayer is survival power. Though the night may come down dark around and the faith with which we face the night seems small, or perhaps no faith at all; yet, if we pray, always some spark leaps up through the tinder of our hearts, a little light to show us our way. Prayer is life. Prayer is a reaching, and every act of prayer stretches the soul. Prayer is spiritual exercise, and we have never uttered a single prayer without having enlarged our spiritual capacity.

Yet, sometimes when I pray I do not need to speak any word at all. I merely need to give myself to God, and God gives Himself to me.

Much of prayer is speaking, yet much of it is listening. And the speaking we do in prayer is important, but the listening is even more important. For it is as we listen that God speaks. And it is when we are still that God acts. It is in the silence that the word of God is uttered and the work of God is done.

Some wonder how they will recognize the word of God. I know only that when God speaks it is in a language you will understand. If it is words, it will be words you know. If it is feelings, you will understand them, too. For feeling is the unforgotten language of the heart; you could speak it before you learned words, the language of the mind.

Prayer is a journey we make into ourselves, a journey we make toward God. We think of ourselves as islands, but we are truly mainlands. Beyond the cape of self lies a continent of being. It is not to our changing mortal self that we must look to understand our meaning and our destiny, but to this larger self-lessness that lies beyond.

True prayer is apprehension of the changeless Truth, which abides at the heart of the changeful world, the Truth of God.

For myself, I have not found the meaning and value of prayer to lie so much in the answer to prayer as in the prayer itself. For prayer is a way of life as well as a way of facing life. It is an end as well as a means. It is a spiritual experience. Prayer is the way of walking with God instead of walking alone. Those who have a habit of prayer are never far from God, even though at times they may lose sight of Him. Because they have the habit of prayer, they often find things changed by their prayers. But even when things do not change they have a sense that all is well. For they have a sense of a sustaining presence—at the heart of things, compassion! Though they may not understand why some things occur, they know that God is there. Therefore, nothing that occurs can be meaningless. They and their lives are meaningful.

So they can accept their lives and themselves, striving to change what they feel is good to change, but accepting what they cannot change in the faith that behind all the events of life God is working out His pattern of divinity.

To those who pray, prayer is life itself!

JAMES DILLET FREEMAN

January

PRAYER FOR EACH DAY

A New Beginning

Let the words of our mouth
    and the meditations of our heart
    be acceptable
        in Your sight, Lord.

You are our strength.

You are our Redeemer.

And if through the words of man
    we hear not
    the voice of God,
        then speak to each of us
            in the quietness
                of our own hearts.
            Amen.

REVEREND RICHARD M. FREEMAN

FLOWER—CARNATION • BIRTHSTONE—GARNET

JANUARY

GENESIS
1, 2, 3, 4

1

MATTHEW
1, 2

PSALM 34:1 **I WILL BLESS THE LORD AT ALL TIMES:** his praise shall continually be in my mouth.

_____
_____
_____
_____
_____

GENESIS
5, 6, 7

2

MATTHEW
3

PSALM 77:6 **I CALL TO REMEMBRANCE MY SONG IN THE NIGHT:** I commune with mine own heart: and my spirit made diligent search.

_____
_____
_____
_____
_____

GENESIS
8, 9, 10

3

MATTHEW
4

PSALM 51:10 **CREATE IN ME A CLEAN HEART, O GOD;** and renew a right spirit within me.

_____
_____
_____
_____
_____

GENESIS
11, 12, 13

4

MATTHEW
5:1-26

PSALM 1:1 **BLESSED IS THE MAN** that walketh not in the council of the ungodly, nor standeth in the way of sinners, nor sitteth in the seat of the scornful.

_____
_____
_____
_____
_____

_____
_____
_____
_____
_____

JANUARY

PSALM 136:1   O Give thanks unto the Lord; for he is good: for HIS MERCY ENDURETH FOR EVER.

_____
_____
_____
_____
_____
_____

PSALM 89:1   I WILL SING OF THE MERCIES OF THE LORD FOR EVER: with my mouth will I make known thy faithfulness to all generations.

_____
_____
_____
_____
_____

PSALM 25:5   LEAD ME IN THY TRUTH, and teach me: for thou art the God of my salvation; on thee do I wait all the day.

_____
_____
_____
_____
_____

PSALM 124:8   OUR HELP IS IN THE NAME OF THE LORD, who made heaven and earth.

_____
_____
_____
_____
_____

_____
_____
_____
_____
_____

JANUARY

PSALM 3:5   I laid me down and slept; I awaked; for THE LORD SUSTAINED ME.

_____

_____

_____

_____

_____

_____

PSALM 37:40   . . . AND THE LORD SHALL HELP THEM, AND DELIVER THEM; he shall deliver them from the wicked, and save them, because they trust in him.

_____

_____

_____

_____

PSALM 23:3   HE RESTORETH MY SOUL: he leadeth me in the paths of righteousness for his name's sake.

_____

_____

_____

_____

_____

PSALM 108:3   I WILL PRAISE THEE, O LORD, among the people: and I will sing praises unto thee among the nations.

_____

_____

_____

_____

_____

_____

_____

_____

_____

_____

_____

JANUARY

PSALM 49:3   **MY MOUTH SHALL SPEAK OF WISDOM** and the meditation of my heart shall be of understanding.

_____
_____
_____
_____
_____
_____

GENESIS
30, 31

13

MATTHEW
9:20-38

PSALM 30:11   **THOU HAST TURNED FOR ME MY MOURNING INTO DANCING:** thou hast put off my sackcloth, and girded me with gladness.

_____
_____
_____
_____
_____
_____

GENESIS
32, 33

14

MATTHEW
10:1-14

PSALM 149:4   . . . For the Lord taketh pleasure in his people: **HE WILL BEAUTIFY THE MEEK WITH SALVATION.**

_____
_____
_____
_____
_____
_____

GENESIS
34, 35

15

MATTHEW
10:15-28

PSALM 70:4   **LET ALL THOSE THAT SEEK THEE REJOICE AND BE GLAD IN THEE:** and let such as love thy salvation say continually, Let God be magnified.

_____
_____
_____
_____
_____
_____

GENESIS
36, 37

16

MATTHEW
10:29-42

JANUARY

A TREASURE FOR THE NEW YEAR is to be glad of life, because it gives you the chance to love and to work and to play and to look up at the stars; to be satisfied with your possessions, but not contented with yourself until you have made the best of them; to despise nothing in the world except falsehood and meanness, and to fear nothing except cowardice; to be governed by your admirations rather than by your disgusts; to covet nothing that is your neighbor's except his kindness of heart and gentleness of manners; to think seldom of your enemies, often of your friends and every day of Christ; and to spend as much time as you can with body and with spirit, in God's out-of-doors, these are little guideposts on the footpath of peace.

HENRY VAN DYKE

PRAYER

You are denying yourself a marvelous privilege if you don't pray. The path of prayer is always open, whatever your need. Take it to the Lord in prayer!

BILLY GRAHAM

THE STUDY OF GOD'S WORD, for the purpose of discovering God's will, is the secret discipline which has formed the greatest characters.

J. W. ALEXANDER

I BEGAN to keep a list of people for whom I wanted to pray. And before I knew it, I discovered that God was touching more and more of my life through this time of prayer.

KEITH MILLER

JESUS' PROMISE to you and me is that the Helper will be with us always, day and night, standing by for any protection we need and for every emergency. Our only part is to recognize His presence and to call upon Him.

Once the truth of this amazing comradeship gets firmly imbedded in our mind and heart, we need never be afraid again, or lonely, or hopeless, or sorrowful, or helplessly inadequate. For the Helper is always with us, and altogether adequate.

CATHERINE MARSHALL

WE ASK OUR DAILY BREAD, and God never says you should have come yesterday, he never says you must go again tomorrow, but today if you will hear his voice, today he will hear you.

JOHN DONNE

. . . WHATEVER HAPPENS, life must go on for you. There are too many friends and loved ones depending on you for it to be otherwise. Whatever happens to us, the stream of life must flow on. So, take good care of yourselves and don't give way to total defeat. Much in life is for you and with you, whatever comes. Keep this firmly fixed, these days.

ROBERT V. OZMENT

WITHOUT LOVE and kindness, life is cold, selfish, and uninteresting, and leads to distaste for everything. With kindness, the difficult becomes easy, the obscure clear; life assumes a charm and its miseries are softened. If we knew the power of kindness, we should transform this world into a paradise.

CHARLES WAGNER

JANUARY

GOOD THOUGHTS are beautiful flowers, promoting good deeds and making others happy, thereby enriching our lives and bringing us happiness.

AUTHOR UNKNOWN

YOU ARE NEEDED

You are needed where you are.
   As in the heavens
      each and every star
      fills appointed space
so you fill the place
      where God has need.
Oh, do not doubt—
   Your hand held out
      to help a friend,
      your love to warm
an empty heart,
      even your smile
      to light the dark.
Walk serene in grace
      you are in your needed place.

ELIZABETH SEARLE LAMB

EARTH has no sorrow that Heaven cannot heal.

THOMAS MOORE

LETTING GO the unworthy things that meet us, pretense, worry, discontent and self-seeking—and taking hold of time, work, present happiness, love, duty, friendship, sorrow, and faith, let us so live in all our relationships as to be an inspiration, strength, and blessing to those whose lives are touched by ours!

AUTHOR UNKNOWN

WHAT DO WE LIVE FOR if it is not to make life less difficult for each other?

GEORGE ELIOT

WHEN GOD DECIDED to break into history with his own character, when he decided to share his love with the world, he decided to do it in personal, not ideological, terms. He came to us as Word in Flesh, Jesus Christ. Jesus Christ is the love of God breaking through and finding us where we really are. If we really want to know what love is, if we really want to get some kind of handle on the love of God, then we must consider Jesus Christ. We must look closely at him in the New Testament. We must watch him in action. Only then will the love of God begin to become clear to us, and only then will it begin to make a difference in our lives.

EARL F. PALMER

WHAT IS LOVELY never dies, but passes into other loveliness.

THOMAS A. ALDRICH

IF I WERE A VOICE

If I were a Voice—a consoling Voice—
   I'd fly on the wings of Air;
The home of Sorrow and Guilt I'd seek
And calm and truthful words I'd speak,
   To save them from Despair.
I'd fly, I'd fly o'er the crowded town,
And drop,
Like the happy sunlight, down
   Into the hearts of suffering men,
   And teach them to rejoice again.

CHARLES MACKAY

WHEN WE CALL ON GOD, He bends down His ear to listen, as a father bends down to listen to his little child. Yes, God listens.

ELIZABETH CHARLES

JANUARY

GENESIS
38, 39

17

MATTHEW
11

PSALM 1:6   **FOR THE LORD KNOWETH THE WAY OF THE RIGHTEOUS:** but the way of the ungodly shall perish.

_____
_____
_____
_____
_____
_____

GENESIS
40, 41

18

MATTHEW
12:1-19

PSALM 48:14   . . . For this God is our God for ever and ever: **HE WILL BE OUR GUIDE EVEN UNTO DEATH.**

_____
_____
_____
_____
_____
_____

GENESIS
42, 43

19

MATTHEW
12:20-38

PSALM 19:9   **THE FEAR OF THE LORD IS CLEAN, ENDURING FOR EVER:** the judgments of the Lord are true and righteous altogether.

_____
_____
_____
_____
_____

GENESIS
44, 45

20

MATTHEW
12:39-50

PSALM 119:16   I will delight myself in thy statutes: **I WILL NOT FORGET THY WORD.**

_____
_____
_____
_____
_____
_____
_____
_____
_____
_____

JANUARY

PSALM 9:13   **HAVE MERCY UPON ME, O LORD;** consider my trouble which I suffer of them that hate me, thou that liftest me up from the gates of death....

_____
_____
_____
_____
_____

PSALM 37:5   **COMMIT THY WAY UNTO THE LORD;** trust also in him; and he shall bring it to pass.

_____
_____
_____
_____
_____
_____

PSALM 56:11   **IN GOD HAVE I PUT MY TRUST: I** will not be afraid what man can do unto me.

_____
_____
_____
_____
_____
_____

PSALM 106:47   **SAVE US, O LORD OUR GOD, and** gather us from among the heathen, to give thanks unto thy holy name, and to triumph in thy praise.

_____
_____
_____
_____
_____
_____
_____
_____

GENESIS
46, 47

21

MATTHEW
13:1-22

GENESIS
48, 49

22

MATTHEW
13:23-44

GENESIS
50

23

MATTHEW
13:45-58

EXODUS
1, 2

24

MATTHEW
14:1-18

JANUARY

EXODUS
3, 4

25

MATTHEW
14:19-36

PSALM 30:2   **O LORD MY GOD, I CRIED UNTO THEE, and thou hast healed me.**

_____
_____
_____
_____
_____
_____

EXODUS
5, 6

26

MATTHEW
15:1-19

PSALM 95:6   **O come, let us worship and bow down: LET US KNEEL BEFORE THE LORD OUR MAKER.**

_____
_____
_____
_____
_____

EXODUS
7, 8

27

MATTHEW
15:20-39

PSALM 96:13   **Before the Lord: for he cometh, for he cometh to judge the earth: HE SHALL JUDGE THE WORLD WITH RIGHTEOUSNESS, AND THE PEOPLE WITH HIS TRUTH.**

_____
_____
_____
_____

EXODUS
9, 10

28

MATTHEW
16

PSALM 2:7   **I will declare the decree: the Lord hath said unto me, THOU ART MY SON; this day have I begotten thee.**

_____
_____
_____
_____

_____
_____
_____
_____
_____

JANUARY

PSALM 18:32   **IT IS GOD THAT GIRDETH ME WITH STRENGTH,** and maketh my way perfect.

EXODUS
11, 12

29

MATTHEW
17

PSALM 27:6   **. . . And now shall mine head be lifted up above mine enemies round about me; therefore will I offer in his tabernacle sacrifices of joy; I WILL SING, YEA, I WILL SING PRAISES UNTO THE LORD.**

EXODUS
13, 14

30

MATTHEW
18:1-17

PSALM 61:1   **Hear my cry, O GOD, ATTEND UNTO MY PRAYER.**

EXODUS
15, 16

31

MATTHEW
18:18-35

FLOWERS FROM PARADISE

The best and sweetest flowers
of paradise
God gives to His people
when they are upon their knees.
Prayer is the gate of heaven.

THOMAS BROOKS

JANUARY

LOOK AT THE CROSS

Father, you are the God of love. When we look at the cross of our Lord Jesus Christ, we see that love poured out for us. What remarkable love that is, love that will not let us go, love that pursues us despite our rebuffs, love that never gives up, is relentless in its pursuit until we yield, broken, melted by your love. Lord, this is the nature and character of the love that is shed abroad in our hearts by the Holy Spirit which is given unto us. It is this remarkable thing that the world waits to see in Christian people. It is the absence of this, Father, that makes them turn away from our doors, uninterested, disappointed. Lord, teach us then to love one another. Whatever this may mean in terms of our personal circumstances, teach us, Father, to love one another. In Christ's name. Amen.

RAY C. STEDMAN

GO FORTH NOBLY

The old year is slipping behind us. We cannot stop it if we would. We must go forth and leave our past. Let us go forth nobly, as those whom great thoughts and greater deeds await beyond. Let us go humbly, solemnly, bravely, as those must go who go to meet the Lord. With firm, quiet, serious steps, full of faith, hope, let us go to meet Him who will certainly judge us when we meet Him, but who loves us while He judges us, and who, if we are obedient, will make us, by the discipline of all the years, fit for the everlasting world, where life shall count itself by years no longer.

PHILLIPS BROOKS

LORD GOD, thank you for coming in Jesus Christ so that I could know who you are and what I was meant to be. Let my heart be broken by the things which break your heart. Remind me that at the end of this day I will have only the things I have given away. Amen.

LLOYD JOHN OGILVIE

Behind the cloud the starlight lurks,
    Through showers the sunbeams fall;
For God who loveth all His works,
    Has left His Hope with all.

JOHN GREENLEAF WHITTIER

OFF AND ON, throughout our day we should be turning quickly to God to praise and thank Him, and to ask for His help. Prayers should be specific. God is interested in everything you do and nothing is too great or too insignificant to share with Him.

BILLY GRAHAM

TO LIVE IN HEARTS we leave behind is not to die.

CAMPBELL

RECONNECTION

Dear Lord, thank you that we're not alone, and that somehow as we try to relate to you, help us to realize that you are alive trying to relate to us. Give us the courage to face you and to face ourselves so that we may come back into a relationship with you that you've shown us is possible in Jesus Christ. Amen.

KEITH MILLER

JANUARY

FOR MY NEIGHBORS

I am so grateful, dear God, for my neighbors—those who are walking the sunset trail of life, those who are well set on the way, and those who are just starting. I am thankful for their thoughtful, helpful, cheerful attitudes toward my family and me. Lord, show me how I, in turn, may be a good neighbor to them.

Help me to use every opportunity to offer words of encouragement and cheer, as well as to show by acts of kindness, the gratitude I feel for them. And, dear Lord, help me at all times to be patient with the children. May I rejoice in their laughter, be interested in their education, pray for their spiritual development, listen to their problems, and make them welcome in my home.

So Father, bless my neighbors and help me to love them. I pray in the name of Jesus, who said, "Love thy neighbour as thyself." Amen.

LOUISE MILLER NOVOTNY

February

HELP ME LIVE FOR OTHERS

The Perfect Prayer

Lord help me live from day to day,
    In such a self-forgetful way,
That even when I kneel to pray
        My prayer shall be for others.

Help me in all the work I do,
    To ever be sincere and true,
And know all that I'd do for You,
        Must needs be done for others.

Let "Self" be crucified and slain,
    And buried deep: all in vain,
My efforts be to rise again,
        Unless to live for others.

And when my work on earth is done,
    And my new work in heaven's begun,
May I forget the crown I've won.
        While thinking still of others.

Others, Lord, yes, others.
    Let this my motto be,
Help me to live for others,
        That I may live like Thee.

CHARLES DELUCENA MEIGS
FROM THE PERSONAL COLLECTION OF RONALD E. GARMAN

FLOWER—PRIMROSE • BIRTHSTONE—AMETHYST

FEBRUARY

EXODUS
17, 18, 19

1

MATTHEW
19

PSALM 1:3 . . . And HE SHALL BE LIKE A TREE planted by the rivers of water, that bringeth forth his fruit in his season, his leaf also shall not wither; and whatsoever he doeth shall prosper.

_____
_____
_____
_____

EXODUS
20, 21, 22

2

MATTHEW
20:1-17

PSALM 37:11 . . . But THE MEEK SHALL INHERIT THE EARTH: and shall delight themselves in the abundance of peace.

_____
_____
_____
_____
_____

EXODUS
23, 24

3

MATTHEW
20:18-34

PSALM 25:7 Remember not the sins of my youth, nor my transgressions: according to thy mercy REMEMBER THOU ME FOR THY GOODNESS' SAKE, O LORD.

_____
_____
_____
_____

EXODUS
25, 26, 27

4

MATTHEW
21:1-20

PSALM 128:1 BLESSED IS EVERY ONE THAT FEARETH THE LORD; that walketh in his ways.

_____
_____
_____
_____
_____
_____
_____
_____

FEBRUARY

PSALM 19:8   The statutes of the Lord are right, rejoicing the heart: THE COMMANDMENT OF THE LORD IS PURE, enlightening the eyes.

_____
_____
_____
_____
_____

EXODUS

28, 29

5

MATTHEW

21:21-46

PSALM 9:7   . . . But THE LORD SHALL ENDURE FOR EVER: he hath prepared his throne for judgment.

_____
_____
_____
_____
_____

EXODUS

30, 31

6

MATTHEW

22:1-20

PSALM 26:8   LORD, I HAVE LOVED THE HABITATION OF THY HOUSE, and the place where thine honour dwelleth.

_____
_____
_____
_____
_____

EXODUS

32, 33

7

MATTHEW

22:21-46

PSALM 105:3   Glory ye in his holy name: LET THE HEART OF THEM REJOICE THAT SEEK THE LORD.

_____
_____
_____
_____
_____

EXODUS

34, 35, 36

8

MATTHEW

23:1-19

FEBRUARY

EXODUS
37, 38

9

MATTHEW
23:20-39

PSALM 38:21 Forsake me not, O Lord: O MY GOD, BE NOT FAR FROM ME.

_____
_____
_____
_____
_____
_____

EXODUS
39, 40

10

MATTHEW
24:1-18

PSALM 2:12 Kiss the Son, lest he be angry, and ye perish from the way, when his wrath is kindled but a little. BLESSED ARE ALL THEY THAT PUT THEIR TRUST IN HIM.

_____
_____
_____
_____

LEVITICUS
1, 2

11

MATTHEW
24:19-38

PSALM 113:3 From the rising of the sun unto the going down of the same THE LORD'S NAME IS TO BE PRAISED.

_____
_____
_____
_____
_____

LEVITICUS
3, 4, 5

12

MATTHEW
25:1-23

PSALM 63:8 My soul followeth hard after thee: THY RIGHT HAND UPHOLDETH ME.

_____
_____
_____
_____
_____
_____
_____
_____
_____
_____

FEBRUARY

PSALM 13:6   **I WILL SING UNTO THE LORD,** because he hath dealt bountifully with me.

_____
_____
_____
_____
_____
_____

LEVITICUS
6, 7, 8

13

MATTHEW
25:24-46

PSALM 6:9   The Lord hath heard my supplication; **THE LORD WILL RECEIVE MY PRAYER.**

_____
_____
_____
_____
_____
_____

LEVITICUS
9, 10

14

MATTHEW
26:1-23

PSALM 25:20   **O KEEP MY SOUL, AND DELIVER ME:** let me not be ashamed; for I put my trust in thee.

_____
_____
_____
_____
_____
_____

LEVITICUS
11, 12

15

MATTHEW
26:24-46

PSALM 104:34   My meditation of him shall be sweet: **I WILL BE GLAD IN THE LORD.**

_____
_____
_____
_____
_____
_____

LEVITICUS
13

16

MATTHEW
27:1-24

_____
_____
_____
_____
_____

FEBRUARY

SMILE THROUGH THE TEARS

All of us live amid a dying world. Death dominates the planet—not just physical death, but also the death of hopes, dreams, ambitions, love, family, friends and a hundred other human aspirations.

Yet in spite of all this decadence and despair life can be beautiful. We can bring comfort, cheer and consolation to our contemporaries. We can be those who weep with those who weep, who smile through the tears with those who smile through their tears.

We can draw near to help people pick up the pieces and make a fresh start. We can bring beauty for ashes. We can share the Spirit of God's joy to replace the spirit of a heavy heart.

W. PHILLIP KELLER

BLESSINGS

Reflect upon your present blessings, of which every man has many; not upon your past misfortunes, of which all men have some.

CHARLES DICKENS

COMPANIONSHIP

The assurance of immortality alone is not enough. For if we are told that we are to live forever and still left without the knowledge of a personal God, eternity stretches before us like a boundless desert, a perpetual and desolate orphanage. It is the Divine companionship that the spirit needs first of all and most deeply.

HENRY VAN DYKE

HAPPINESS

It's not so much the world outside
That makes us sigh or smile—
It's more the thoughts within our hearts
That make life seem worthwhile!

And often on a day like this,
I wonder if you guess,
How many times the thought of you
Has brought me happiness!

AUTHOR UNKNOWN

GOD has two dwellings: one in Heaven, and the other in a meek and thankful heart.

IZAAK WALTON

GIVING

Do right, and God's recompense to you will be the power of doing more right. Give, and God's reward to you will be the spirit of giving more: a blessed spirit, for it is the Spirit of God Himself, whose Life is the blessedness of giving. Love, and God will pay you with the capacity of more love; for love is Heaven —love is God within you.

F. W. ROBERTSON

HE WHO GIVES HIMSELF

It is he who gives himself to let the love of God dwell in him, and in the practice of daily life to love as God loves, who will have the power to believe in the love that will hear his every prayer. It is the Lamb who is in the midst of the throne; it is suffering and forbearing love that prevails with God in prayer.

ANDREW MURRAY

FEBRUARY

Ofttimes when the highway of life
    seems rough
And all of your dreams have flown,
    Just remember,
wherever your road may go . . .
    Nobody walks alone.
When everyone else has let you down
    And under your sins you groan,
    Just keep reminding
      your burdened heart . . .
Nobody walks alone.
Then suddenly you'll feel
    His hand in yours
And His eyes lifting up your own
    And you'll hear His gentle,
      forgiving voice . . .

    "Nobody walks alone."
      NICK KENNY

A BEAUTIFUL DAY'S a mixture of work
and play and joy and love.
    AUTHOR UNKNOWN

RISK EVERYTHING

Give Him a chance in your life. Prepare
your own heart and just see what's
going to happen to you. I would challenge you to commit your life totally to
Him and decide to do something that
you and I both know needs to be done
and that is a surrender of your talents,
your gifts God has given you and a surrender of your past and the sins that
you know have been hindering a relationship with Christ. I'd like to encourage you to step out and risk everything
you have for the Lord. 'Cause once you
do that, you know He's just going to
load on the blessings.
    EVIE

WE GIVE THEE THANKS

For spreading plain and peak that towers,
    We give Thee thanks.
For sun and rain and food and flowers,
    We give Thee thanks.

For courage and the will to do,
For strength and hope and faith anew,
For love and friendship fond and true,
    We give Thee thanks.
For pain that serves to purge the soul,
    We give Thee thanks.
For cares that raise us toward the goal,
    We give Thee thanks.

For bits of rest that intervene,
For tears and signs, with smiles between,
For all the good that life can mean,
    We give Thee thanks.
    AUTHOR UNKNOWN

THE ART OF GIVING

We give of ourselves when we give gifts
of the heart: love, kindness, joy, understanding, sympathy, tolerance, forgiveness . . .

We give of ourselves when we give gifts
of the mind: ideas, dreams, purposes,
ideals, principles, plans, inventions,
projects, poetry . . .

We give of ourselves when we give gifts
of the spirit: prayer, vision, beauty,
aspiration, peace, faith . . .

The finest gift a man can give to his age
and time is the gift of a constructive and
creative life.
    WILFERD A. PETERSON

FEBRUARY

LEVITICUS
14

17

MATTHEW
27:25-50

PSALM 27:14   WAIT ON THE LORD: be of good courage, and he shall strengthen thine heart: wait, I say, on the Lord.

_____
_____
_____
_____
_____

LEVITICUS
15, 16

18

MATTHEW
27:51-66

PSALM 61:8   SO WILL I SING PRAISE UNTO THY NAME FOR EVER, that I may daily perform my vows.

_____
_____
_____
_____
_____

LEVITICUS
17, 18

19

MATTHEW
28

PSALM 24:5   HE SHALL RECEIVE THE BLESSINGS FROM THE LORD, and righteousness from the God of his salvation.

_____
_____
_____
_____

LEVITICUS
19, 20

20

MARK
1:1-21

PSALM 43:3   O SEND OUT THY LIGHT AND THY TRUTH: let them lead me; let them bring me into thy holy hill, and to thy tabernacles.

_____
_____
_____
_____

_____
_____
_____
_____

FEBRUARY

PSALM 18:1 I WILL LOVE THEE, O LORD, my strength.

_____
_____
_____
_____
_____
_____

LEVITICUS
21

21

MARK
1:22-45

PSALM 69:32 The humble shall see this, and be glad: and YOUR HEART SHALL LIVE THAT SEEK GOD.

_____
_____
_____
_____
_____

LEVITICUS
22, 23

22

MARK
2

PSALM 40:11 Withhold not thou thy tender mercies from me, O Lord: LET THY LOVINGKIND-NESS AND THY TRUTH CONTINUALLY PRESERVE ME.

_____
_____
_____
_____

LEVITICUS
24, 25

23

MARK
3:1-17

PSALM 54:6 I will freely sacrifice unto thee: I WILL PRAISE THY NAME, O LORD: FOR IT IS GOOD.

_____
_____
_____
_____
_____

LEVITICUS
26, 27

24

MARK
3:18-35

_____
_____
_____
_____
_____

FEBRUARY

NUMBERS
1, 2

25

MARK
4:1-21

PSALM 5:2   Hearken unto the voice of my cry, my King, and my God: for UNTO THEE WILL I PRAY.

_____
_____
_____
_____
_____
_____

NUMBERS
3, 4

26

MARK
4:22-41

PSALM 21:5   HIS GLORY IS GREAT IN THY SALVATION: honour and majesty hast thou laid upon him.

_____
_____
_____
_____
_____
_____

NUMBERS
5, 6, 7

27

MARK
5:1-21

PSALM 113:2   BLESSED BE THE NAME OF THE LORD from this time forth and for evermore.

_____
_____
_____
_____
_____
_____

NUMBERS
8, 9

28

MARK
5:22-43

PSALM 100:3   KNOW YE THAT THE LORD HE IS GOD: it is he that hath made us, and not we ourselves; we are his people, and the sheep of his pasture.

_____
_____
_____
_____

_____
_____
_____
_____
_____

FEBRUARY

TRUE FRIENDSHIP

I love you not only for what you are, but for what I am when I am with you. I love you not only for what you have made of yourself, but for what you are making of me. I love you for the part of me you bring out. I love you for putting your hand in my heart and passing over all the weak things that you cannot help seeing; and drawing out into the light all the beautiful radiant things that no one else has looked quite far enough to find. I love you for ignoring the possibilities of the fool in me and for laying firm hold of the possibilities of the good in me. I love you for closing your ears to the discord in me by worshipful listening; I love you because you are helping me to make of the lumber of my life not a tavern but a temple, and the words of my everyday not a reproach but a song. I love you because you have done more than any creed could have done to make me happy. You have done it without a touch, without a word, without a sign; you have done it by just being yourself. Perhaps that is what being a friend means after all.

AUTHOR UNKNOWN

FEBRUARY

I AM WILLING LORD

Sometimes when I am down,
And I don't feel like
    You're around, O Lord.
Feeling so sorry for me
Not knowing that all the while
    You're working to see;
If when I am put through the fire,
I'll come out shining like gold.
O Lord, please don't ever stop
    working with me,
'Till You see I can be
All You want me to be.

I am willing, Lord, I am willing, Lord

To be just exactly
    what You want me to be.

I am willing, Lord, I am willing, Lord

To be just exactly
    what You want me to be.

Often when I ask "Why,"
Teach me then on You to rely,
    O Lord.
You surely know what is best,
May I learn that in confidence and
    strength I can rest.
Then, leaning fully on You,
My questions fall one by one.
Dear Lord, please don't ever stop
    working with me,
'Till You see I can be
All You want me to be.

                 KURT KAISER

ONE MAY GIVE without loving;
    but none can love without giving.
                AUTHOR UNKNOWN

THE CREATION

All things bright and beautiful,
    All creatures, great and small,
All things wise and wonderful,
    The Lord God made them all.

Each little flower that opens,
    Each little bird that sings,
He made their glowing colors,
    He made their tiny wings:

The rich man in his castle,
    The poor man at his gate,
God made them, high or lowly,
    And ordered their estate.

The purple-headed mountain,
    The river running by,
The sunset and the morning,
    That brightens up the sky;

The cold wind in the winter,
    The pleasant summer sun,
The ripe fruits in the garden—
    He made them every one.

The tall trees in the greenwood,
    The meadows where we play,
The rushes by the water
    We gather every day—

He gave us eyes to see them,
    And lips that we might tell
How great is God Almighty,
    Who has made all things well!
        CECIL FRANCES ALEXANDER

LOVE does not mean one thing in man
and another in God . . . . The divine
heart is human in its sympathies.
              F. W. ROBERTSON

FEBRUARY

THE HEAVENS DECLARE THE GLORY OF GOD

You ask me how I know it's true
   That there is a living God—
A God who rules the universe,
   The sky . . . the sea . . . the sod;
A God who holds all creatures
   In the hollow of His hand;
A God who put Infinity
   In one tiny grain of sand;
A God who made the seasons—
   Winter, Summer, Fall and Spring,
And put His flawless rhythm
   Into each created thing;
A God who hangs the sun out
   Slowly with the break of day,
And gently takes the stars in
   And puts the night away;
A God whose mighty handiwork
   Defies the skill of man,
For no architect can alter
   God's Perfect Master Plan—
What better answers are there
   To prove His Holy Being
Than the wonders all around us
   That are ours just for the seeing.

HELEN STEINER RICE

March

THANK YOU, LORD

A Beautiful Prayer of Surrender

Oh God, there are people now who are opening their minds and hearts to receive and accept Jesus Christ into their life. Thank You, God, thank You. He's more alive than ever before. In the years that have passed since He lived and died, today more people on planet earth believe in Him than have ever lived on this earth at one time before. Thank You, Lord. Make me a true follower, now. Let my mind be a mind through which Christ can think, my face a face through which Christ can smile, my lips a tongue through which He can speak, my heart a heart through which He can love, my hand a hand which He can use to reach out and help a stumbling friend. In His name we pray. Amen.

ROBERT SCHULLER

FLOWER—VIOLET • BIRTHSTONE—BLOODSTONE

MARCH

NUMBERS

10, 11

1

MARK

6:1-27

PSALM 118:28   THOU ART MY GOD, AND I WILL PRAISE THEE: thou art my God, I will exalt thee.

_____

_____

_____

_____

_____

_____

NUMBERS

12, 13

2

MARK

6:28-56

PSALM 12:6   THE WORDS OF THE LORD ARE PURE WORDS: as silver tried in a furnace of earth, purified seven times.

_____

_____

_____

_____

_____

NUMBERS

14, 15

3

MARK

7:1-18

PSALM 57:5   BE THOU EXALTED, O GOD, above the heavens: let thy glory be above all the earth.

_____

_____

_____

_____

_____

NUMBERS

16, 17

4

MARK

7:19-37

PSALM 18:6   IN MY DISTRESS I CALLED UPON THE LORD, and cried unto my God: he heard my voice out of his temple, and my cry came before him, even into his ears.

_____

_____

_____

_____

_____

_____

_____

_____

_____

MARCH

PSALM 25:13   HIS SOUL SHALL DWELL AT EASE; and his seed shall inherit the earth.

_____
_____
_____
_____
_____
_____

NUMBERS

18, 19

5

MARK

8:1-19

PSALM 34:14   DEPART FROM EVIL, AND DO GOOD; seek peace, and pursue it.

_____
_____
_____
_____
_____
_____

NUMBERS

20, 21

6

MARK

8:20-38

PSALM 66:4   ALL THE EARTH SHALL WORSHIP THEE, and shall sing unto thee; they shall sing to thy name.

_____
_____
_____
_____
_____

NUMBERS

22, 23

7

MARK

9:1-25

PSALM 3:3   . . . But THOU, O LORD, ART A SHIELD FOR ME; my glory, and the lifter up of mine head.

_____
_____
_____
_____
_____

NUMBERS

24, 25

8

MARK

9:26-50

_____
_____
_____
_____
_____

MARCH

NUMBERS

26, 27

9

MARK

10:1-25

PSALM 37:34   WAIT ON THE LORD, and keep his way, and he shall exalt thee to inherit the land: when the wicked are cut off, thou shalt see it.

NUMBERS

28, 29, 30

10

MARK

10:26-52

PSALM 86:7   IN THE DAY OF MY TROUBLE I WILL CALL UPON THEE: for thou wilt answer me.

NUMBERS

31, 32, 33

11

MARK

11:1-16

PSALM 22:26   The meek shall eat and be satisfied: they shall praise the Lord that seek him: YOUR HEART SHALL LIVE FOR EVER.

NUMBERS

34, 35, 36

12

MARK

11:17-33

PSALM 59:17   Unto thee, O my strength, will I sing: FOR GOD IS MY DEFENCE, AND THE GOD OF MY MERCY.

MARCH

PSALM 31:5   INTO THINE HAND I COMMIT MY SPIRIT: thou hast redeemed me, O Lord God of truth.

_____
_____
_____
_____
_____
_____

DEUTERONOMY
1, 2, 3

13

MARK
12:1-22

PSALM 84:4   BLESSED ARE THEY THAT DWELL IN THY HOUSE: they will be still praising thee.

_____
_____
_____
_____
_____
_____

DEUTERONOMY
4, 5, 6

14

MARK
12:23-44

PSALM 72:17   HIS NAME SHALL ENDURE FOR EVER: his name shall be continued as long as the sun: and men shall be blessed in him: all nations shall call him blessed.

_____
_____
_____
_____

DEUTERONOMY
7, 8, 9

15

MARK
13:1-18

PSALM 145:13   THY KINGDOM IS AN EVER-LASTING KINGDOM, and thy dominion endureth throughout all generations.

_____
_____
_____
_____
_____

DEUTERONOMY
10, 11, 12

16

MARK
13:19-37

_____
_____
_____
_____
_____

MARCH

THE RESURRECTION of Jesus Christ on that first Easter morning meant that death was conquered once and for all, and it was indeed the fulfillment of His promise . . .

FLOYD THATCHER

BEAUTY

Beauty is of the soul,
    A thing that is felt, not seen . . .
A sort of inner glow
    That comes from a spirit serene.

Beauty is really truth . . .
    A thing that time can't consume . . .
Whereas loveliness without virtue
    Is a flower without perfume.

The handsomest features fade
    As time takes its cruel toll,
But sweeter the person grows
    When beauty is of the soul.

NICK KENNY

LOVE is the doorway through which the human soul passes from selfishness to service and from solitude to kinship with all mankind.

AUTHOR UNKNOWN

KEEP THE FIRES BURNING

Jesus, I want a fire in my soul for God. Jesus, I want to strike sparks in the hearts of my children that will light their way into a family of their own. Jesus, I want something in me so discernible and so appealing that my children will want to keep the fires of their father burning. Thank you, Lord.

REVEREND RICHARD M. FREEMAN

WHEN THE CLOUDS of sorrow begin to descend, one may be tempted to discard his faith and walk alone, but the wise person will turn to God for strength and help. Helen Keller wrote, "I, too, have loved and lost; I, too, must often fight hard to keep a steadfast faith. When I fail to hear the Divine Voice, grief overwhelms me, my faith wavers; but I must not let it go, for without faith there would be no light in the world. Faith lifts up shining arms and points to a happier world where our loved ones await us."

ROBERT V. OZMENT

IT IS NOT EASY to be a great soul, and possibly most of us are not very keen to be one. But evidently Almighty God wants us to be of this caliber; and upon some, of whom he desires real greatness of soul, he confers the creative experience of pain.

NORMAN VINCENT PEALE

KINDNESS

Kindness is not a prominent Christian virtue today, when all of us seem so intent on our own courses and accomplishments. It's an almost forgotten art to put others before self—just to be kind. But in every fellowship of believers, we encounter the individual (or individuals) who goes out of his way to show love, who shows his Christianity by his kindness or consideration for others, reflecting as in a mirror that marvelous Christlike spirit which is to be our pattern. It is God who is the Source of this, our kindness.

AL BRYANT

MARCH

EASTER MORNING

Tomb, thou shalt not hold him longer:
Death is strong, but life is stronger;
Stronger than the dark, the light;
Stronger than the wrong, the right;
Faith and hope triumphant say,
"Christ will rise on Easter Day!"

While the patient earth lies waking
Till the morning shall be breaking,
Shuddering 'neath the burden dread
Of her Master, cold and dead,
Hark! she hears the angels say,
"Christ will rise on Easter Day!"

And when sunrise smites the mountains,
Pouring light from heavenly fountains,
Then the earth blooms out to greet
Once again the blessed feet;
And her countless voices say:
"Christ has risen on Easter Day!"

PHILLIPS BROOKS

GOD makes very sure that the principle of sowing and reaping never falters. And on the basis of His commitments to us we may be perfectly certain that any act or deed of kindness we show in mercy and compassion to another, will eventually be returned to us in rich and abundant compensation. We harvest what is planted. And when seeds of kindness are sown prayerfully in the garden plot of our lives we may be sure there will be a bountiful harvest of blessings for both us and others. Life can become exceedingly rich in benefits this way.

W. PHILLIP KELLER

When in sorrow, read JOHN 14.

GIVE US COURAGE and gaiety and the quiet mind. Spare us to our friends, soften us to our enemies. Bless us, if it may be, in our innocent endeavors. If it may not be, give us strength to encounter that which is to come, that we be brave in peril, constant in tribulation, temperate in wrath, and in all changes of fortune, and down to the gates of death, loyal and loving one another. As the clay to the potter, as the windmill to the wind, as children to their sire, we beseech of Thee this help and mercy.

Let peace abound in our small company. Purge out of every heart the lurking grudge. Give us grace and strength to forbear and persevere. Offenders, give us the grace to accept and forgive offenders. Forgetful of ourselves, help us to bear cheerfully the forgetfulness of others.

ROBERT LOUIS STEVENSON

LOVE . . . the golden key that opens the palace of eternity.

JOHN MILTON

UNLESS THE HEART IS KIND

Your kindness was much more
    Than words to feed my mind
For words are meaningless
    Unless the heart is kind.
And you can never grasp
    How much your kindness blessed
Till one encourages you
    When you're gripped with distress.
Your thoughtful words to me
    And deeds remembered yet
Because your heart is kind
    I never will forget.

PERRY TANKSLEY

MARCH

DEUTERONOMY

13, 14, 15

17

MARK

14:1-26

PSALM 119:145   I CRIED WITH MY WHOLE HEART; HEAR ME, O LORD: I will keep thy statutes.

_____
_____
_____
_____
_____
_____

DEUTERONOMY

16, 17, 18

18

MARK

14:27-54

PSALM 5:3   MY VOICE SHALT THOU HEAR IN THE MORNING, O Lord; in the morning will I direct my prayer unto thee, and will look up.

_____
_____
_____
_____
_____

DEUTERONOMY

19, 20, 21

19

MARK

14:55-72

PSALM 67:3   LET THE PEOPLE PRAISE THEE, O GOD; let all the people praise thee.

_____
_____
_____
_____
_____

DEUTERONOMY

22, 23, 24

20

MARK

15:1-28

PSALM 25:18   Look upon mine affliction and my pain: and FORGIVE ALL MY SINS.

_____
_____
_____
_____
_____

_____
_____
_____
_____
_____

MARCH

PSALM 31:24   **BE OF GOOD COURAGE,** and he shall strengthen your heart, all ye that hope in the Lord.

_____
_____
_____
_____
_____

DEUTERONOMY
25, 26, 27

21

MARK
15:29-47

PSALM 103:1   **BLESS THE LORD, O MY SOUL:** and all that is within me, bless his holy name.

_____
_____
_____
_____
_____

DEUTERONOMY
28, 29

22

MARK
16

PSALM 32:11   **BE GLAD IN THE LORD,** and rejoice, ye righteous: and shout for joy, all ye that are upright in heart.

_____
_____
_____
_____
_____

DEUTERONOMY
30, 31

23

LUKE
1:1-19

PSALM 90:12   **So TEACH US TO NUMBER OUR DAYS,** that we may apply our hearts unto wisdom.

_____
_____
_____
_____
_____

DEUTERONOMY
32, 33, 34

24

LUKE
1:20-40

_____
_____
_____
_____
_____

MARCH

JOSHUA
1, 2, 3, 4

25

LUKE
1:41-60

PSALM 100:2   **SERVE THE LORD WITH GLAD-
NESS: come before his presence with singing.**

_____
_____
_____
_____
_____
_____

JOSHUA
5, 6, 7

26

LUKE
1:61-80

PSALM 7:17   **I WILL PRAISE THE LORD according to his righteousness: and will sing praise to the
name of the Lord most high.**

_____
_____
_____
_____
_____

JOSHUA
8, 9, 10

27

LUKE
2:1-25

PSALM 33:5   **He loveth righteousness and judgment: THE EARTH IS FULL OF THE GOODNESS OF
THE LORD.**

_____
_____
_____
_____
_____

JOSHUA
11, 12, 13

28

LUKE
2:26-52

PSALM 89:16   **IN THY NAME SHALL THEY
REJOICE ALL THE DAY: and in thy righteousness
shall they be exalted.**

_____
_____
_____
_____

_____
_____
_____
_____

MARCH

PSALM 29:4   The voice of the Lord is powerful, **THE VOICE OF THE LORD IS FULL OF MAJESTY.**

_____
_____
_____
_____
_____
_____

JOSHUA
14, 15, 16

29

LUKE
3

PSALM 34:4   **I SOUGHT THE LORD, AND HE HEARD ME,** and delivered me from all my fears.

_____
_____
_____
_____
_____
_____

JOSHUA
17, 18, 19

30

LUKE
4:1-22

PSALM 86:5   . . . for **THOU, LORD, ART GOOD, AND READY TO FORGIVE;** and plenteous in mercy unto all them that call upon thee.

_____
_____
_____
_____
_____
_____

JOSHUA
20, 21, 22

31

LUKE
4:23-44

LIFE BECOMES RICHER

In looking for specific things to thank God for each morning I began to see His hand everywhere, and life became richer and filled with good things.

KEITH MILLER

_____
_____
_____
_____
_____
_____

MARCH

THE FORMULA for cooperating with God is this: To love God is to let God love you; to let God love you is to be completely open to what he wants to do in every part of your thinking, feeling, and attitude.

LLOYD JOHN OGILVIE

THANKFULNESS

I'm thankful for the dawn of day,
For useful work and buoyant play;
I'm thankful for the faith of friends,
For humble heart that condescends.

I'm thankful for the trees and flowers,
For sapphire seas and cooling showers;
I'm thankful for the world of books,
For chanting birds and purling brooks.
I'm thankful for the sun at noon,
For silent stars and crescent moon;
I'm thankful for the gift of prayer,
For blessings I can freely share.

I'm thankful for the right to live,
For daily chance to serve and give;
I'm thankful most to God above
For His protecting, perfect love.

GRENVILLE KLEISER

NO MAN is an island, entire of itself; every man is a piece of the continent, a part of the main.

JOHN DONNE

. . . READING the Scriptures every day and having a specific time of prayer for the cultivation of a real and dynamic relationship with Christ are the two things that become most meaningful and real.

KEITH MILLER

POSTLUDE

The pageantry of Easter Day . . .
Has come and gone again . . .
The hope of life beyond the grave . . .
Has been retold to men . . .
And we must all come back again . . .
To daily tasks at hand . . .
To teaching school and keeping shop . . .
And farming our good land . . .
Yet as we do resume our work . . .
In ordinary things . . .
Let's keep the glory in our tasks . . .
Which Easter always brings . . .
Let's count our many blessings . . .
The large ones and the small . . .
And then bow down to thank our God,
Who blesses one and all.

ALICE KENNELLY ROBERTS

THE LESSON OF LOSS

Thank you, God, for the wonderful lesson of loss.

The arms of my friends console me, the love of my family surrounds me. The goodness and kindness of my neighbors sustain me like a staff.

Though I am prostrate with grief I am supported, as by a great shining column that rises up within me. I can lift up my head, I can walk upright. I can even smile.

For their sympathy is also like a lovely pool in which I see glimpses of goodness and beauty never revealed before. In it my agony is soothed, the ache of my heart becomes bearable and will, I know, one day heal.

MARJORIE HOLMES

When in doubt, read JOHN 7:17.

MARCH

GOD SETS NO SEASON

God sets no season for the wind to blow
Or hearts to swell with gratitude and praise;
With lavish hand, from planting time to snow,
He scatters bounty through our hours and days.

Fruits mellow on each orchard tree, each vine
That sprawls along a winding country lane;
Each spider-web and star, in its design,
Offers rare beauty, plentiful as rain.

The heart that overflows with thankfulness
Will be enriched beyond imagining,
And from its store of love find ways to bless
Others who need its care and cherishing.

God sets no season for the soul to sing;
The caring heart enjoys perpetual spring.

ALICE MACKENZIE SWAIM

April

STRENGTH
FOR EACH DAY

The Promise of God's Love

God hath not promised
  Skies always blue . . .

Flower-strewn pathways
  All our lives through.

God hath not promised
  Sun without rain . . .

Joy without sorrow,
  Peace without pain.

But God hath promised
  Strength for the day . . .

Rest for the laborer,
  Light for the way.

Grace for the trials,
  Help from above . . .

Unfailing sympathy,
  Undying love.

ANNIE JOHNSON FLINT
FROM THE PERSONAL COLLECTION OF RONALD E. GARMAN

FLOWER—SWEET PEA • BIRTHSTONE—DIAMOND

APRIL

JOSHUA
23, 24

1

LUKE
5:1-19

PSALM 34:15 THE EYES OF THE LORD ARE UPON THE RIGHTEOUS, and his ears are open unto their cry.

_____
_____
_____
_____
_____

JUDGES
1, 2

2

LUKE
5:20-39

PSALM 84:12 O Lord of hosts, BLESSED IS THE MAN THAT TRUSTETH IN THEE.

_____
_____
_____
_____
_____

JUDGES
3, 4

3

LUKE
6:1-14

PSALM 104:24 O Lord, how manifold are thy works! in wisdom hast thou made them all: THE EARTH IS FULL OF THY RICHES.

_____
_____
_____
_____
_____

JUDGES
5, 6

4

LUKE
6:15-29

PSALM 55:22 CAST THY BURDEN UPON THE LORD, and he shall sustain thee: he shall never suffer the righteous to be moved.

_____
_____
_____
_____
_____

APRIL

PSALM 46:10   **BE STILL, AND KNOW THAT I AM GOD;** I will be exalted among the heathen, I will be exalted in the earth.

_____
_____
_____
_____
_____

JUDGES
7, 8

5

LUKE
6:30-49

PSALM 111:10   **THE FEAR OF THE LORD IS THE BEGINNING OF WISDOM:** a good understanding have all they that do his commandments: his praise endureth for ever.

_____
_____
_____
_____

JUDGES
9, 10

6

LUKE
7:1-18

PSALM 37:7   **REST IN THE LORD,** and wait patiently for him: fret not thyself because of him who prospereth in his way, because of the man who bringeth wicked devices to pass.

_____
_____
_____
_____

JUDGES
11, 12

7

LUKE
7:19-34

PSALM 5:8   **LEAD ME, O LORD,** in thy righteousness because of mine enemies; make thy way straight before my face.

_____
_____
_____
_____

JUDGES
13, 14

8

LUKE
7:35-50

_____
_____
_____
_____
_____

APRIL

JUDGES
15, 16

9

LUKE
8:1-14

PSALM 45:2   Thou art fairer than the children of men: grace is poured into thy lips: THEREFORE GOD HATH BLESSED THEE FOR EVER.

_____
_____
_____
_____
_____

JUDGES
17, 18

10

LUKE
8:15-28

PSALM 116:12   WHAT SHALL I RENDER UNTO THE LORD for all his benefits toward me?

_____
_____
_____
_____
_____

JUDGES
19, 20, 21

11

LUKE
8:29-40

PSALM 18:35   THOU HAST ALSO GIVEN ME THE SHIELD OF THY SALVATION: and thy right hand hath holden me up, and thy greatness hath made me great.

_____
_____
_____
_____

RUTH
1, 2

12

LUKE
8:41-50

PSALM 62:7   In God is my salvation and my glory: the rock of my strength, and MY REFUGE, IS IN GOD.

_____
_____
_____
_____

_____
_____
_____
_____
_____

APRIL

PSALM 36:7   **HOW EXCELLENT IS THY LOVING KINDNESS, O GOD!** therefore the children of men put their trust under the shadow of thy wings . . . .

_____
_____
_____
_____
_____

PSALM 121:2   **MY HELP COMETH FROM THE LORD,** which made heaven and earth.

_____
_____
_____
_____
_____
_____
_____

PSALM 57:11   Be thou exalted, O God, above the heavens: **LET THY GLORY BE ABOVE ALL THE EARTH.**

_____
_____
_____
_____
_____

PSALM 145:17   **THE LORD IS RIGHTEOUS IN ALL HIS WAYS,** and holy in all his works.

_____
_____
_____
_____
_____

_____
_____
_____
_____

RUTH
3, 4

13

LUKE
9:1-18

1 SAMUEL
1, 2, 3

14

LUKE
9:19-36

1 SAMUEL
4, 5

15

LUKE
9:37-50

1 SAMUEL
6, 7, 8

16

LUKE
9:51-62

APRIL

WHATEVER FORM IT TAKES, prayer is that solemn moment when the soul in need turns to God.

HUGH McLELLAN

When dawn awakens,
    and when the sweet
        day closes
Deep in my heart
    there linger thoughts
        of you!

CLIFTON BINGHAM

AS WE BEGIN TO LIVE and walk in the Spirit, we find that each wonderful gift He gives us is a sample of that which will be multiplied a thousandfold in the life to come.

There, we shall love as He loves; here, we have a small measure of that love for Him and for each other.

There, we will have the joy of unbroken communion with that amazingly provocative, magnificent Personality; here, only moments and facets of His presence are real to us.

There, we shall have full knowledge; here, the Spirit of Truth gives us bits of knowledge, perception, wisdom, and guidance.

CATHERINE MARSHALL

PRAYER is not conquering God's reluctance, but taking hold upon God's willingness.

PHILLIPS BROOKS

JOY comes in your heart when you have the purifying hope of looking forward to your Savior's return. The joy is indescribable.

JONI EARECKSON

WHERE THE RAINBOW NEVER FADES

It cannot be that the earth is man's only abiding place. It cannot be that our life is a mere bubble cast up by Eternity to float a moment on its waves and then sink into Nothingness. Else why is it that the glorious aspirations which leap like angels from the temple of our hearts are forever wandering unsatisfied? Why is it that all the stars that hold their festival around the midnight throne, are set above the grasp of our limited faculties, forever mocking us with their unapproachable glory? And, finally, why is it that bright forms of human beauty presented to our view are taken from us, leaving the thousand streams of our affections to flow back in Alpine torrents upon our hearts?

There is a realm where the rainbow never fades; where the stars will be spread out before us like islands that slumber in the ocean; and where the beautiful beings which now pass before us like shadows will stay in our presence forever.

GEO. D. PRENTICE

THROUGH JESUS CHRIST, God offers the gift of Himself to us. Imagine! Almighty God, the creator and fashioner of the universe is actually here with us now, cares deeply about both our joys and hurts, and is approachable.

REUBEN JOB

QUIETNESS comes from the presence of peace in the life, not from material gain. Sow the seed of peace and reap the harvest of quiet.

AL BRYANT

APRIL

PRAYER FOR WORSHIP

This week we may be given
    challenges instead of ease,
        courage instead of contentment,
           opportunities instead of rest.

But we have a Savior who brings
    strength out of service,
        faith out of struggle,
           and victory out of defeat.

Go then, fearful of nothing,
    sure that in everything,
        we are held secure
           in the Master's steadfast love.
           Amen.

E. LEE PHILLIPS

I'LL BE LIVING PROOF

Dear God, who made all things
    And made most things appear
To grow in elegance
    With every passing year,
Please beautify my life
    And crown it with Thy grace
So that old age finds me
    Reflecting Jesus' face,
And glorifying Thee
    So that when I grow old
None thinks of seeing me
    But sees Christ in my soul.
If You should grant me this
    And by Thy Presence strengthen
Then I will fear no more
    When evening shadows lengthen.
But I'll be living proof
    That if one does his duty
You'll keep Your promise, God,
    To touch old age with beauty.

PERRY TANKSLEY

TODAY IS OURS

We live but once. The years of childhood, when once past, are past for ever. It matters not how ardently we may wish to live them over; it avails us nothing. So it is with the other stages of life. The past is no longer ours. It has gone beyond our reach. What we have made it, it shall remain. There is no power in Heaven or on earth that can change it. The record of our past stands forth in bold and ineffaceable characters, open to the all-seeing eye of God. There it stands, and one day we shall give an account of it. The present moment alone is ours. "Now is thy treasure possessed unawares." Today is a day which we never had before, which we shall never have again. It rose from the great ocean of eternity, and again sinks into its unfathomable depths.

TALMAGE

HE LOVES each one of us, as if there were only one of us.

SAINT AUGUSTINE

PRAYER FOR THE DAY: Gracious God, thank you for offering us the magnificent gift of peace. In the quiet we want to confess the things that keep us from peace. Help us to accept your forgiveness, forgive ourselves, and express forgiveness to others. We commit our lives to love others as you have loved us. Abide in us, dear God, and love through us. Thank you for the peace that is beyond our understanding, which floods our hearts right now. In Christ's name and power. Amen.

LLOYD JOHN OGILVIE

APRIL

PSALM 71:21   Thou shalt increase my greatness, and COMFORT ME ON EVERY SIDE.

_____

_____

_____

_____

_____

_____

PSALM 16:1   PRESERVE ME, O GOD: for in thee do I put my trust.

_____

_____

_____

_____

_____

_____

PSALM 4:1   HEAR ME WHEN I CALL, O GOD of my righteousness: thou hast enlarged me when I was in distress; have mercy upon me, and hear my prayer.

_____

_____

_____

_____

PSALM 37:39   . . . but THE SALVATION OF THE RIGHTEOUS IS OF THE LORD: he is their strength in the time of trouble.

_____

_____

_____

_____

_____

_____

_____

_____

APRIL

PSALM 8:1   O LORD OUR LORD, how excellent is thy name in all the earth! who hast set thy glory above the heavens.

_____
_____
_____
_____
_____

1 SAMUEL
21, 22, 23

21

LUKE
11:36-54

PSALM 37:27   DEPART FROM EVIL, and do good; and dwell for evermore.

_____
_____
_____
_____
_____

1 SAMUEL
24, 25

22

LUKE
12:1-29

PSALM 13:5   . . . I have trusted in thy mercy; MY HEART SHALL REJOICE IN THY SALVATION.

_____
_____
_____
_____
_____

1 SAMUEL
26, 27, 28

23

LUKE
13

PSALM 28:7   THE LORD IS MY STRENGTH AND MY SHIELD; my heart trusted in him, and I am helped: therefore my heart greatly rejoiceth; and with my song will I praise him.

_____
_____
_____

1 SAMUEL
29, 30, 31

24

LUKE
14

_____
_____
_____
_____

APRIL

2 SAMUEL

1, 2, 3

25

LUKE

15:1-16

PSALM 118:17   I SHALL NOT DIE, BUT LIVE, and declare the works of the Lord.

_____
_____
_____
_____
_____
_____
_____

2 SAMUEL

4, 5, 6

26

LUKE

15:17-32

PSALM 7:1   O LORD MY GOD, IN THEE DO I PUT MY TRUST: save me from all them that persecute me, and deliver me.

_____
_____
_____
_____
_____
_____

2 SAMUEL

7, 8, 9

27

LUKE

16

PSALM 43:4   Then will I go unto the altar of God, unto God my exceeding joy; YEA, UPON THE HARP WILL I PRAISE THEE, O GOD MY GOD.

_____
_____
_____
_____
_____

2 SAMUEL

10, 11

28

LUKE

17:1-18

PSALM 23:2   He maketh me to lie down in green pastures: HE LEADETH ME BESIDE THE STILL WATERS.

_____
_____
_____
_____
_____

_____
_____
_____
_____
_____
_____

APRIL

PSALM 27:4   One thing have I desired of the Lord, that will I seek after, THAT I MAY DWELL IN THE HOUSE OF THE LORD ALL THE DAYS OF MY LIFE, to behold the beauty of the Lord, and to enquire in his temple.

2 SAMUEL
12, 13

29

LUKE
17:19-37

_____
_____
_____

PSALM 50:15   . . . And call upon me in the day of trouble: I WILL DELIVER THEE, AND THOU SHALT GLORIFY ME.

2 SAMUEL
14, 15

30

LUKE
18:1-22

_____
_____
_____
_____

HE IS ETERNAL

He is our Lord. Without Him there would be no praise. He is Yahweh, the great I Am That I Am. He is eternal. He has always been and will always be. He is omniscient. He knows all things in my life and yours. No thought or deed is hidden from Him. He is omnipotent. His power is limitless. Nothing is impossible with Him. No request is too large or too small. He is omnipresent. He is working in every life, wooing us and drawing us to Himself. He is not limited in any way—not in time, nor space, nor power, nor wisdom, nor knowledge.

ANNE MURCHISON

_____
_____
_____
_____
_____
_____
_____

APRIL

I AM only one,
But still I am one.

I cannot do everything,
But still I can do something;
And because I cannot do everything
I will not refuse to do the something
    that I can do.

EDWARD EVERETT HALE

AN EASTER MEDITATION

Dear Lord, in the world of Yesterdays I buried a kindly thought about my neighbors; in the same tomb I laid a high and holy inspiration.

    Once in the days gone by I dreamed a wonderful dream, but some way in the push and bustle of material things the dream was lost, and after a time it also became entombed with other high ideals.

    Today, Lord, because it is the Eastertime, help me to roll the stone away and reveal my better self.

    If any dream of mine has been buried because it seemed too beautiful for realization, resurrect that dream, O Lord, and help me to reveal all that is kind, and holy, and lovely in my life.

BEULAH G. SQUIRES

WE CANNOT KNOW what our dreams really mean until we mix them with those of someone we love.

AUTHOR UNKNOWN

THE ART OF LOVE

The art of love is God at work through you.

WILFERD A. PETERSON

LOVE, says the New Testament, grows out of the decision God made. Love was involved in his decision to create the world, to create mankind, and to redeem individual men and women. All along, love has been his decision. And at a particular point in the course of human history he made that love the central pivotal point of all time. Jesus Christ is that decision-event. He is the love of God. And that love came to us when we weren't even looking for it. It is even called by a special name in the New Testament text: *agapé.*

EARL F. PALMER

BEAUTY seen is never lost.

JOHN GREENLEAF WHITTIER

Do you know the world is dying
    For a little bit of love?
Everywhere we hear them sighing
    For a little bit of love.

For a love that rights a wrong,
    Fills the heart with hope and song.
They have waited, oh, so long,
    For a little bit of love.

While the souls of men are dying
    For a little bit of love;
While the children, too, are crying
    For a little bit of love;

Stand no longer idly by,
    You can help them, if you try;
Go then, saying, "Here am I,
    With a little bit of love."

SELECTED

1 TIMOTHY 1:15 Christ Jesus came into the world to save sinners.

APRIL

THE GIFT OF FRIENDS

The most priceless gift
        that I ever knew
Is the gift of Friends
        the tried and true.
I liken each one to a precious gem,
        A sparkling jewel in a diadem.
Or I think of my friends
        As an endless chain;
The longer it grows,
        as more friends I gain.
Each friend is a link,
        each link a part
        Of a gold chain
        that entwines my heart.
My every prayer begins and ends,
        "I thank Thee, God,
        for the gift of Friends."

EDNA THORNBURG

May

HOW CAN I / TELL YOU FATHER

The Blessing of New Life

How can I tell you Father?
    How can I let you know,
About the new life
      you've planted here
    Where nothing else would grow?

I caught the scent of water,
    The air alive and free,
The smell of spring,
      the warmth of earth, and rain,
    When you breathed on me.

How can I tell you Father?
    How can I let you hear,
The quiet sound
      your clear voice made
    In the traffic of my fears?

I caught a glimpse of stillness,
    The sun was at the sea,
But you were there
      to guard the gate of night
    When you breathed on me.

How can I tell you Father?
    How can I let you know,
About the new life
      you've planted here
    Where nothing else would grow?

How can I tell you Father,
    With song, or tongue or moan,
That you've made this
      anxious desert heart
a garden and a home . . . . .
    When you breathed on me.

KEITH MILLER
COPYRIGHT 1980 KEITH MILLER FROM "JOSEPH LOVES MARY"

FLOWER—LILY OF THE VALLEY • BIRTHSTONE—EMERALD

MAY

2 SAMUEL
16, 17, 18

1

LUKE
18:23-43

PSALM 2:11 SERVE THE LORD with fear, and rejoice with trembling.

_____
_____
_____
_____
_____
_____
_____

2 SAMUEL
19, 20

2

LUKE
19:1-24

PSALM 25:4 Show me thy ways, O LORD; TEACH ME THY PATHS.

_____
_____
_____
_____
_____
_____
_____

2 SAMUEL
21, 22

3

LUKE
19:25-48

PSALM 121:1 I WILL LIFT UP MINE EYES UNTO THE HILLS, from whence cometh my help.

_____
_____
_____
_____
_____
_____
_____

2 SAMUEL
23, 24

4

LUKE
20:1-23

PSALM 83:1 KEEP NOT THOU SILENCE, O GOD: hold not thy peace, and be not still, O God.

_____
_____
_____
_____
_____
_____
_____
_____
_____

MAY

PSALM 25:11   For thy name's sake, O LORD, **PARDON MINE INIQUITY;** for it is great.

_____
_____
_____
_____
_____
_____

1 KINGS
1, 2, 3

5

LUKE
20:24-47

PSALM 9:9   **THE LORD ALSO WILL BE A REFUGE FOR THE OPPRESSED,** a refuge in times of trouble.

_____
_____
_____
_____
_____

1 KINGS
4, 5, 6

6

LUKE
21:1-18

PSALM 135:1   Praise ye the Lord. **PRAISE YE THE NAME OF THE LORD;** praise him, O ye servants of the Lord.

_____
_____
_____
_____
_____

1 KINGS
7, 8, 9

7

LUKE
21:19-38

PSALM 75:1   **UNTO THEE, O GOD, DO WE GIVE THANKS,** unto thee do we give thanks: for that thy name is near thy wondrous works declare.

_____
_____
_____
_____
_____

1 KINGS
10, 11, 12

8

LUKE
22:1-35

MAY

1 KINGS
13, 14, 15

9

LUKE
22:36-71

PSALM 117:2   For his merciful kindness is great toward us: and THE TRUTH OF THE LORD ENDURETH FOR EVER. Praise ye the Lord.

_____
_____
_____
_____
_____

1 KINGS
16, 17, 18

10

LUKE
23:1-27

PSALM 150:6   Let every thing that hath breath praise the Lord. PRAISE YE THE LORD.

_____
_____
_____
_____
_____

1 KINGS
19, 20

11

LUKE
23:28-56

PSALM 18:46   THE LORD LIVETH; and blessed be my rock, and let the God of my salvation be exalted.

_____
_____
_____
_____
_____

1 KINGS
21, 22

12

LUKE
24:1-26

PSALM 37:18   THE LORD KNOWETH THE DAYS OF THE UPRIGHT: and their inheritance shall be for ever.

_____
_____
_____
_____
_____

_____
_____
_____
_____
_____

MAY

PSALM 79:13 So WE THY PEOPLE AND SHEEP OF THY PASTURE WILL GIVE THEE THANKS FOR EVER: we will shew forth thy praise to all generations.

_____
_____
_____
_____

2 KINGS
1, 2, 3

13

LUKE
24:27-53

PSALM 18:21 For I HAVE KEPT THE WAYS OF THE LORD, and have not departed from my God.

_____
_____
_____
_____
_____

2 KINGS
4, 5, 6

14

JOHN
1:1-26

PSALM 37:29 THE RIGHTEOUS SHALL INHERIT THE LAND, and dwell therein for ever.

_____
_____
_____
_____
_____

2 KINGS
7, 8, 9

15

JOHN
1:27-51

PSALM 31:7 I WILL BE GLAD AND REJOICE IN THY MERCY: for thou hast considered my trouble; thou hast known my soul in adversities . . . .

_____
_____
_____
_____

2 KINGS
10, 11, 12

16

JOHN
2

_____
_____
_____
_____

MAY

A PSALM OF LIFE

Life is real! Life is earnest!
    And the grave is not its goal;
Dust thou art, to dust returnest,
    Was not spoken of the soul.

Not enjoyment, and not sorrow,
    Is our destined end or way;
But to act, that each tomorrow
    Find us farther than today.

Lives of great men all remind us
    We can make our lives sublime,
And, departing, leave behind us
    Footprints on the sands of time.

Footprints, that perhaps another,
    Sailing o'er life's solemn main,
A forlorn and shipwrecked brother,
    Seeing, shall take heart again.

I long for household voices gone,
    For vanished smiles I long,
But God hath led my dear ones on,
    And He can do no wrong.

No offering of my own I have,
    Nor works my faith to prove;
I can but give the gifts He gave,
    And plead His love for love.

And so beside the Silent Sea
    I wait the muffled oar;
No harm from Him can come to me
    On ocean or on shore.

I know not where His islands lift
    Their fronded palms in air;
I only know I cannot drift
    Beyond His love and care.

And Thou, O Lord! by whom are seen
    Thy creatures as they be,
Forgive me if too close I lean
    My human heart to Thee!

HENRY WADSWORTH LONGFELLOW

LET US GIVE

When two individuals meet, so do two private worlds. None of our private worlds is big enough for us to live a wholesome life in. We need the wider world of joy and wonder, of purpose and venture, of toil and tears. What are we, any of us, but strangers and sojourners forlornly wandering through the nighttime until we draw together and find the meaning of our lives in one another, dissolving our fears in each other's courage, making music together and lighting torches to guide us through the dark? We belong together. Love is what we need. To love and to be loved. Let our hearts be open; and what we would receive from others, let us give. For what is given still remains to bless the giver—when the gift is love.

A. POWELL DAVIS

THE ETERNAL GOODNESS

O friends! with whom my feet have trod
    The quiet aisles of prayer,
Glad witness to your zeal for God
    And love of man I bear . . .

. . . Ye see the curse which overbroods
    A world of pain and loss;
I hear our Lord's beatitudes
    And prayer upon the cross.

JOHN GREENLEAF WHITTIER

MAY

LORD JESUS, I am busy as a result of conscious choices of what I think is important. Forgive me when my schedule precludes people in need of comfort. I want to live by your agenda. I yield this day and its schedule to you. I believe there is enough time to do the things you will for me to do. Amen.

LLOYD JOHN OGILVIE

NO LONELY HOURS

Lonely hours should never crowd us
　　into depths of deep despair.
Nor should pity overwhelm us,
　　bringing more than we can bear.
We should always leave the shadows,
　　seek the sunshine of a smile;
Never is a day so darkened
　　that the hours are not worth while.

AUTHOR UNKNOWN

THE LOVING DEED

Love demands the loving deed,
　　Pass it on!
Look upon your brother's need—
　　Pass it on!
Live for self, you live in vain;
Live for Christ, with Him you reign—
　　Pass it on!

AUTHOR UNKNOWN

When at last the day is over
　　And we kneel to say a prayer,
We thank God for His blessings,
　　And His tender, loving care.
We thank Him for the woodland,
　　For the sunshine, and the rain;
But most of all we thank Him
　　That we're safe at home again.

ETHEL HILLIARY

I SHALL NOT PASS THIS WAY AGAIN

"O soul, be happy; soon 'tis trod,
The path made thus for thee by God.
Be happy, thou, and bless His name
By whom such marvelous beauty came."
And let no chance by me be lost
To kindness show at any cost.
I shall not pass this way again;
Then let me now relieve some pain,
Remove some barrier from the road,
Or brighten someone's heavy load;
A helping hand to this one lend,
Then turn some other to befriend.
　　　O God, forgive
　　　　That now I live
As if I might, sometime, return
To bless the weary ones that yearn
For help and comfort every day—
For there be such along the way.
O God, forgive that I have seen
The beauty only, have not been
Awake to sorrow such as this;
That I have drunk the cup of bliss
Remembering not that those there be
Who drink the dregs of misery.
For those who tread on rock and stone,
And bear their burdens all alone,
Who loiter not in leafy bowers,
Nor hear the birds or pluck the flowers.
A larger kindness give to me,
A deeper love and sympathy;
　　　Then, O, one day
　　　　May someone say—
Remembering a lessened pain—
"Would she could pass this way again."

EVA ROSE YORK

IN SICKNESS let me not so much say, am I getting better of my pain, but rather, am I getting better for it?

SHAKESPEARE

MAY

PSALM 23:1   **THE LORD IS MY SHEPHERD: I** shall not want.

_____
_____
_____
_____
_____
_____

PSALM 37:4   Delight thyself also in the Lord, and **HE SHALL GIVE THEE THE DESIRES OF THINE HEART.**

_____
_____
_____
_____
_____

PSALM 141:3   **SET A WATCH, O LORD, BEFORE MY MOUTH;** keep the door of my lips.

_____
_____
_____
_____
_____

PSALM 4:8   I will both lay me down in peace, and sleep: **FOR THOU, LORD, ONLY MAKEST ME DWELL IN SAFETY.**

_____
_____
_____
_____

_____
_____
_____
_____
_____

MAY

PSALM 5:11 . . . But let all those that put their trust in thee rejoice: let them ever shout for joy, because thou defendest them: LET THEM ALSO THAT LOVE THY NAME BE JOYFUL IN THEE.

2 KINGS
21, 22

21

JOHN
5:1-23

PSALM 116:9 I WILL WALK BEFORE THE LORD in the land of the living.

2 KINGS
23, 24

22

JOHN
5:24-47

PSALM 17:8 KEEP ME AS THE APPLE OF THE EYE, hide me under the shadow of thy wing . . . .

2 KINGS
25

23

JOHN
6:1-24

PSALM 23:6 Surely goodness and mercy shall follow me all the days of my life: AND I WILL DWELL IN THE HOUSE OF THE LORD FOR EVER.

1 CHRONICLES
1, 2, 3

24

JOHN
6:25-50

MAY

1 CHRONICLES
4, 5, 6

25

JOHN
6:51-71

PSALM 26:11   . . . But as for me, I will walk in mine integrity: REDEEM ME, AND BE MERCIFUL UNTO ME.

_____
_____
_____
_____
_____

1 CHRONICLES
7, 8, 9

26

JOHN
7:1-26

PSALM 54:2   HEAR MY PRAYER, O GOD; give ear to the words of my mouth.

_____
_____
_____
_____
_____

1 CHRONICLES
10, 11, 12

27

JOHN
7:27-53

PSALM 86:3   BE MERCIFUL UNTO ME, O LORD: for I cry unto thee daily.

_____
_____
_____
_____
_____

1 CHRONICLES
13, 14, 15

28

JOHN
8:1-28

PSALM 35:9   . . . AND MY SOUL SHALL BE JOYFUL IN THE LORD: it shall rejoice in his salvation.

_____
_____
_____
_____
_____
_____
_____
_____

MAY

PSALM 19:7 THE LAW OF THE LORD IS PER-FECT, converting the soul: the testimony of the Lord is sure, making wise the simple.

_____
_____
_____
_____
_____

PSALM 38:22 Make haste to help me, O LORD MY SALVATION.

_____
_____
_____
_____
_____
_____

PSALM 23:4 Yea, though I walk through the valley of the shadow of death, I WILL FEAR NO EVIL: FOR THOU ART WITH ME; thy rod and thy staff they comfort me.

_____
_____
_____
_____

IN TIME OF NEED

Let us therefore come boldly unto the throne of grace, that we may obtain mercy, and find grace to help in time of need.

HEBREWS 4:16

_____
_____
_____
_____
_____
_____
_____

MAY

Never a day goes by
But something new I see—
It may be a newborn flower
Or a bird on the tip of a tree.

Never a day goes by
But something new I hear—
It may be the call of a child
And her laughter sweet and clear.

Never a day goes by
But something new I touch—
It may be the hand of a friend
Of one I love so much.

Never a day goes by
But something new I know—
The blessing of strength restored
For the way God would have me go.

AUTHOR UNKNOWN

WHERE there is a human being there is
an opportunity for kindness.

SENECA

IN THE QUIET OF THE MORNING

In the quiet of the morning,
 Oh, how sweet it is to come
Just to talk a bit with Jesus
 Ere the crowding duties come.

Just to kneel there for a moment
 With your head upon His breast,
All your problems laid before Him,
 Every human need confessed.

Oh, the loving strength that surges
 From His heart to yours all day;
Like a bright and shining armor,
 Just because you knelt to pray!

ALICE H. MORTENSON

WE'VE LIVED AND LOVED TOGETHER

We have lived and loved together
Through many changing years;
We have shared each other's gladness
And wept each other's tears;
I have known ne'er a sorrow
That was long unsoothed by thee;
For thy smiles can make a summer
Where darkness else would be.

Like the leaves that fall around us
In autumn's fading hours,
Are the traitor's smiles, that darken
When the cloud of sorrow lowers;
And though many such we've known,
Love too prone, alas, to range,
We both can speak of one love
Which time can never change.

We have lived and loved together
Through many changing years;
We have shared each other's gladness.
And wept each other's tears.
And let us hope the future,
As the past has been will be:
I will share with thee my sorrows,
And thou thy joys with me.

CHARLES JEFFERYS

COMMIT TO GOD the one you have lost,
along with yourself. God knows how to
take care of His own.

 I wish I had a magic word to wipe
away your tears! I do not know any
magic words, but I know a God who can
heal you and I commend Him to you.
Remember, the door of death is the only
door that leads to the Father's house. He
will be waiting there to greet and welcome His children.

ROBERT V. OZMENT

MAY

FAITH

The Shepherd knows what pastures are best for His sheep, and they must not question nor doubt, but trustingly follow Him. Perhaps He sees that the best pastures for some of us are to be found in the midst of opposition or of earthly trials. If He leads you there, you may be sure they are green for you, and you will grow and be made strong by feeding there. Perhaps He sees that the best waters for you to walk beside will be raging waves of trouble and sorrow. If this should be the case, He will make them still waters for you, and you must go and lie down beside them, and let them have all their blessed influences upon you.

H. W. SMITH

June

YOUR LOVE IS A GRACE FOR ME

Your Love Has Made a Place for Me

Every hour I rejoice in Your Love.
The nights of renewed peace
   You have given me . . .
You console my heart and set my spirit free.
I face each day with a new awareness . . .
Because Your Love strengthens me.

Your Love is a grace for me;
Your Love has made a place for me.

Because I thought I could do it all
   on my own . . .
I realize all the moments I've wasted.
Many days slipped away
   as I failed on my own . . .
Then at my darkest hour
   a gentle love filled my heart.
It was then I knew You touched me.

Your Love is a grace for me,
Your Love has made a place for me.

Help me to do what pleases You.
When I die unto myself and forsake my greed . . .
You . . . You alone will provide
   for my every need.
My faith is the seed that only You can sow.
It blossoms with Your glow.

Your Love is a grace for me,
Your Love has made a place for me.

You never promised me
   a life without sorrow and pain . . .
And both come as surely as the rain.
But with the rain comes renewal . . .
My renewal came from Your love and pain.
As I grow old and feeble with wear . . .
Help me to always remember that You care.
When my time comes . . . this I know . . .
Your Love, sweet Jesus, will only grow.

Your Love is a grace for me,
Your Love has made a place for me.

When my life is over and
   the sunshine of this life is gone.
I will be singing Your song, Lord . . .
   Your Song . . .
Help my friends, family and
   loved ones be aware . . .
That for them You also care.
And when we meet in Your Heavenly home . . .
My soul will rejoice because I know . . .

Your Love is a grace for me,
Your Love has made a place for me.

RONALD E. GARMAN

FLOWER—ROSE • BIRTHSTONE—PEARL

JUNE

1 CHRONICLES

25, 26

1

JOHN

10:1-22

PSALM 18:28   **FOR THOU WILT LIGHT MY CANDLE: the Lord my God will enlighten my darkness.**

_____
_____
_____
_____
_____
_____

1 CHRONICLES

27, 28, 29

2

JOHN

10:23-42

PSALM 100:5   For the Lord is good; his mercy is everlasting; and **HIS TRUTH ENDURETH TO ALL GENERATIONS.**

_____
_____
_____
_____

2 CHRONICLES

1, 2, 3, 4

3

JOHN

11:1-28

PSALM 37:37   **MARK THE PERFECT MAN, and** behold the upright: for the end of that man is peace.

_____
_____
_____
_____
_____
_____

2 CHRONICLES

5, 6

4

JOHN

11:29-57

PSALM 57:7   My heart is fixed, O God, my heart is fixed: **I WILL SING AND GIVE PRAISE.**

_____
_____
_____
_____
_____
_____
_____

JUNE

PSALM 4:5   Offer the sacrifices of righteousness, and PUT YOUR TRUST IN THE LORD.

_____
_____
_____
_____
_____
_____
_____

2 CHRONICLES
7, 8, 9

5

JOHN
12:1-24

PSALM 51:2   Wash me throughly from mine iniquity, AND CLEANSE ME FROM MY SIN.

_____
_____
_____
_____
_____
_____
_____

2 CHRONICLES
10, 11, 12

6

JOHN
12:25-50

PSALM 106:1   Praise ye the Lord, O GIVE THANKS UNTO THE LORD; for he is good: for his mercy endureth for ever.

_____
_____
_____
_____
_____
_____

2 CHRONICLES
13, 14

7

JOHN
13:1-19

PSALM 61:8   SO WILL I SING PRAISE UNTO THY NAME FOR EVER, that I may daily perform my vows.

_____
_____
_____
_____
_____
_____

2 CHRONICLES
15, 16, 17

8

JOHN
13:20-38

_____
_____
_____
_____
_____

JUNE

---

2 CHRONICLES

18

9

JOHN

14, 15

PSALM 116:1   I LOVE THE LORD, because he hath heard my voice and my supplications.

_____
_____
_____
_____
_____
_____

---

2 CHRONICLES

19

10

JOHN

16, 17

PSALM 17:15   AS FOR ME, I WILL BEHOLD THY FACE IN RIGHTEOUSNESS: I shall be satisfied, when I awake, with thy likeness.

_____
_____
_____
_____
_____

---

2 CHRONICLES

20, 21

11

JOHN

18:1-20

PSALM 119:105   THY WORD IS A LAMP UNTO MY FEET, and a light unto my path.

_____
_____
_____
_____
_____
_____

---

2 CHRONICLES

22, 23

12

JOHN

18:21-40

PSALM 30:12   To the end that my glory may sing praise to thee, and not be silent. O Lord my God, I WILL GIVE THANKS UNTO THEE FOR EVER.

_____
_____
_____
_____
_____
_____
_____
_____

JUNE

PSALM 6:4   **RETURN, O LORD, DELIVER MY SOUL:** oh save me for thy mercies' sake.

_____
_____
_____
_____
_____
_____

PSALM 29:2   Give unto the Lord the glory due unto his name: **WORSHIP THE LORD IN THE BEAUTY OF HOLINESS.**

_____
_____
_____
_____
_____

PSALM 133:1   Behold, how good and how pleasant it is for brethren to **DWELL TOGETHER IN UNITY.**

_____
_____
_____
_____
_____

PSALM 37:23   **THE STEPS OF A GOOD MAN ARE ORDERED BY THE LORD:** and he delighteth in his way.

_____
_____
_____
_____
_____
_____
_____

2 CHRONICLES
24, 25

13

JOHN
19:1-21

2 CHRONICLES
26, 27

14

JOHN
19:22-42

2 CHRONICLES
28, 29

15

JOHN
20, 21

2 CHRONICLES
30, 31

16

ACTS
1

JUNE

LET US BE QUIET

It is only through quiet meditation that we can correct our judgments, deepen our knowledge, and formulate wise plans. By means of meditation we rise above "the babel of voices" and learn to appraise our ideas and opinions at their true value. In inward silence and stillness, we learn to know and to do the will of God.

AUTHOR UNKNOWN

CHRISTIAN PRAYER inevitably drives a person, sooner or later, out of the privacy of his or her soul, beyond the circle of his or her little group of Christian friends and across the barriers between social, racial, and economic strata to find the wholeness, the real closeness of Christ in that involvement with the lives of His lost and groping children, whoever and wherever they may be.

KEITH MILLER

THE ART OF AWARENESS is enlarging the scope of your life through the expansion of your personality.

WILFERD A. PETERSON

THE GREATEST THING, says someone, a man can do for his heavenly Father is to be kind to some of His other children. I wonder why it is we are not all kinder than we are? How much the world needs it. How easily it is done. How instantaneously it acts. How infallibly it is remembered. How superabundantly it pays itself back—for there is no debtor in the world so honorable, so superbly honorable, as love.

HENRY DRUMMOND

O ETERNAL GOD: We bring Thee our children. They were Thine but Thou in love didst lend them to us for a little season: to care for, to love and to cherish. It has been a labor of love and has seemed but a few days because of the affection we bear them. Fresh from Thy hand they were, in the morning of their lives. Clean and upright, but yet two separate personalities. Tonight we give them back to Thee—no longer as two—but as one flesh. May nothing short of death dissolve the union here cemented. And to this end let the marvelous grace of God do its perfect work!

JAMES C. DOBSON, SR.

LOVE doesn't consist of looking only at each other, but in looking outward together, in the same direction.

AUTHOR UNKNOWN

GIVE TO THE WORLD

Salt is neither showy nor spectacular! Salt is not strident! It is simple. It is silent. Yet it is special in its healing qualities.

He simply asks us to be those silent, sincere souls who in service to Him and those around us help to heal a hurting, broken world.

We can bring to this sick world honest work, inspiring hope, good cheer, lofty ideals, a helping hand, a warm heart, a shining smile, a word of encouragement, a friendly hug, a share of ourselves.

Because we have been here some broken heart, some broken home or some broken hope will have been healed. And even God will be glad.

W. PHILLIP KELLER

JUNE

DO YOU HAVE a physical family? Then snuggle close together for warmth, food, and love hopefully provided there. But recognize that your true source of godly love, warmth, nourishment, and togetherness should come from the larger family, the eternal family. Look carefully at the emphasis in the New Testament epistles, God's directions for us in this church age. They tell us to use our gifts to nourish the Body of Christ, and to draw our nourishment from the Body, so that all the adult singles, young people without Christian parents, and marrieds without Christian spouses will feel just as cared for and loved and nourished as anyone else in God's beautiful forever-family. And when we're loved and fed and prayed for there, our lacks and needs in our physical family relationships will be wonderfully met.

ANNE ORTLUND

The heart has its own memory
          like the mind,
And in it are enshrined the precious
          keepsakes, into which is wrought
The giver's loving thought.

HENRY WADSWORTH LONGFELLOW

BEFORE THE THRESHOLD OF MY DAY

I've much to do today, dear Lord,
          But let me kneel a bit
Before the threshold of my day,
          That I may enter it
With mind serene and heart made fresh
          With fragrant heavenly dew,
That every moment of the day
          I'll be reflecting You.

ALICE H. MORTENSON

THE ANSWER

If you would ask the why
          that I should love you
Through all the years and
          weeks and days and hours,
Then I would ask why do you
          love the springtime
And all the beauty of its
          trees and flowers?
If you would ask again why
          I should love you,
Pretending all the time
          you cannot see,
Then I would say because
          you are my springtime,
The one God made one day
          and gave to me!

GEORGE L. EHRMAN

I CAN AFFIRM from experience that allowing the Helper to guide one's life is an exciting, fulfilling way to live. His plans for each of us are so startlingly superior to anything we can imagine.

CATHERINE MARSHALL

REJOICE

Rejoice! The summons to rejoice is sounded no less than seventy times in the New Testament. There is a vast difference between pleasure and Christian joy. Pleasure depends on circumstances, but Christian joy is completely independent of health, money, or surroundings. When circumstances are against you, when every modern comfort is withdrawn, you may still experience the miracle of joy produced by the Holy Spirit who lives within.

BILLY GRAHAM

JUNE

2 CHRONICLES
32, 33

17

ACTS
2:1-24

PSALM 23:5   Thou preparest a table before me in the presence of mine enemies: thou anointest my head with oil; MY CUP RUNNETH OVER.

_____
_____
_____
_____
_____

2 CHRONICLES
34, 35, 36

18

ACTS
2:25-47

PSALM 19:14   Let the words of my mouth, and the meditation of my heart, be acceptable in thy sight, O LORD, MY STRENGTH, AND MY REDEEMER.

_____
_____
_____
_____

EZRA
1, 2, 3

19

ACTS
3

PSALM 107:1   O give thanks unto the Lord, for he is good: for HIS MERCY ENDURETH FOR EVER.

_____
_____
_____
_____
_____

EZRA
4, 5, 6

20

ACTS
4:1-18

PSALM 36:9   . . . FOR WITH THEE IS THE FOUNTAIN OF LIFE: in thy light shall we see light.

_____
_____
_____
_____
_____
_____

_____
_____
_____
_____
_____

JUNE

PSALM 66:1 **MAKE A JOYFUL NOISE UNTO GOD,** all ye lands.

_____
_____
_____
_____
_____
_____

EZRA

7, 8, 9

21

ACTS

4:19-37

PSALM 31:23 **O LOVE THE LORD,** all ye his saints: for the Lord preserveth the faithful, and plentifully rewardeth the proud doer.

_____
_____
_____
_____
_____
_____

EZRA

10

22

ACTS

5:1-21

PSALM 112:1 Praise ye the Lord. **BLESSED IS THE MAN THAT FEARETH THE LORD,** that delighteth greatly in his commandments.

_____
_____
_____
_____
_____

NEHEMIAH

1, 2

23

ACTS

5:22-42

PSALM 40:16 **LET ALL THOSE THAT SEEK THEE REJOICE AND BE GLAD IN THEE:** let such as love thy salvation say continually, The Lord be magnified.

_____
_____
_____
_____

NEHEMIAH

3, 4

24

ACTS

6

_____
_____
_____
_____
_____

JUNE

25

PSALM 64:10   THE RIGHTEOUS SHALL BE GLAD IN THE LORD, and shall trust in him; and all the upright in heart shall glory.

_____
_____
_____
_____
_____

26

PSALM 5:1   GIVE EAR TO MY WORDS, O LORD, consider my meditation.

_____
_____
_____
_____
_____
_____
_____

27

PSALM 25:6   REMEMBER, O LORD, THY TENDER MERCIES and thy loving kindnesses; for they have been ever of old.

_____
_____
_____
_____
_____

28

PSALM 115:18   . . . But we will bless the Lord from this time forth and for evermore. PRAISE THE LORD.

_____
_____
_____
_____
_____
_____

_____
_____
_____
_____
_____

JUNE

PSALM 145:8   THE LORD IS GRACIOUS, and full of compassion; slow to anger, and of great mercy.

ESTHER
1, 2, 3

29

ACTS
8:21-40

_____
_____
_____
_____
_____
_____

PSALM 22:27   ALL THE ENDS OF THE WORLD SHALL REMEMBER AND TURN UNTO THE LORD: and all the kindreds of the nations shall worship before thee.

ESTHER
4, 5, 6

30

ACTS
9:1-21

_____
_____
_____
_____

I AM MORE

I am more than happy; I am joyful.
I am more than healthy; I am whole.
I am more than alive; I am radiant.
I am more than successful; I am free.
I am more than caring; I am loving.
I am more than tranquil; I am peaceful.
I am more than interested; I am involved.
I am more than adequate; I am triumphant.
I am more than fortunate; I am prosperous.
I am more than human; I am a child of
     God.

WILLIAM ARTHUR WARD

_____
_____
_____
_____
_____
_____
_____
_____

JUNE

IT IS BY GRACE, God's unmerited favor, that we win the battle of being faithful without losing the war of being effective. If we ask him, he will give us people in our structures with whom we can share the delight of being alive in Christ, and also by grace, he will give us decision-making power to influence the lives of others.

LLOYD JOHN OGILVIE

IF YOU ARE LOOKING for a model of service to follow, Jesus Christ is the supreme example that the Scriptures give us, as to what a Christian servant should be. Always busy, He was also completely dependent upon His heavenly Father for every step of His way. His prayer life is an inspiration to believers, for He did not take a step without communicating to His God.

AL BRYANT

SIMPLE JOYS

Gracefully grow older with the
    simple joys of each passing day . . .
A smile, word or touch from others
    are simple joys that come your way . . .
Dream your dreams of tomorrow
    but make the beauty of today last . . .
Let today touch your heart
    with the simple joys of the past.

RONALD E. GARMAN

BLESSED are they who have the gift of making friends, for it is one of God's best gifts. It involves many things, but, above all, the power of going out of one's self, and seeing and appreciating what is noble and loving in another.

THOMAS HUGHES

WORSHIPFUL BEAUTY

The most beautiful world is always enticed through the imagination. The splendor of the sunset my friends gaze at across the purpling hills, is wonderful, but the sunset of the inner vision brings purer delight because it is the worshipful blending of all the beauty that we have known or desired.

HELEN KELLER

HAPPINESS is not perfected until it is shared.

J. PETIT SENN

AMAZING GRACE

Amazing grace! how sweet the sound,
    That saved a wretch like me!
I once was lost, but now am found,
    Was blind, but now I see.

'Twas grace that taught my heart to fear,
    And grace my fears relieved;
How precious did that grace appear
    The hour I first believed!

Thro' many dangers, toils and snares,
    I have already come;
'Tis grace hath bro't me safe thus far
    And grace will lead me home.

When we've been there ten thousand years,
    Bright shining as the sun,
We've no less days to sing God's praise
    Than when we first begun.

JOHN NEWTON

MAY WE, God helping us, be part of the answer, not part of the problem.

PETER MARSHALL

JUNE

BEFORE IT IS TOO LATE

If you have a tender message,
      Or a loving word to say,
Do not wait till you forget it,
      But whisper it today;
The tender word unspoken,
      The letter never sent,
The long forgotten messages,
      The wealth of love unspent—
For these some hearts are breaking,
      for these some loved ones wait;
So show them that you care for them
      Before it is too late.

FRANK HERBERT SWEET

July

FRESH GRACE FOR EACH DAY

The Reassurance of God's Amazing Grace

The other morning a friend startled me with a greeting which became like a time-release capsule throughout the day. "A gracious day to you!" he said. I thought about that all day. It exploded with healing, strength, and courage all through the day. A gracious day is one filled with fresh experiences of God's grace.

Gracious means filled with grace. Each day can be the best day of our lives when we receive and communicate grace. Grace is what God is and gives. Grace is not static but dynamic. It is the personal gift of the Spirit of God. Grace is the Divine energy rolling in like a mighty ocean on the shores of human need. By grace we are loved just as we are. Grace is unmotivated love given in spite of sin and failure. It is unqualified forgiveness even before we ask, motivating us to desire the loving kindness God is more ready to give than we are to ask. Grace spells God's intervention in all our needs. He invades our circumstances with unlimited power. The amazing grace of God is that He knows and cares about each of us as if there were only one of us.

Christ is the grace of God with us. John caught the wonder of that. "And of His fullness we have received, and grace for grace." The Greek really means, "grace instead of grace" or "grace in exchange for grace." Christ brought grace beyond the law. The grace of the Lord Jesus offers us reconciling love through the cross. We no longer need to justify ourselves. We are free! There is grace which reconciles and grace which releases. Grace which redeems and grace to risk. Grace for eternal life to live forever, and grace for the abundant life to live without reservation today. But "grace for grace" also means that we can depend on fresh grace each day. Our problems are but a prelude to new grace to exceed anything we've known before.

Nothing is impossible when we live by grace. We become channels, riverbeds, of grace to others. We can be gracious in our relationships as our hearts are filled with God's heart to overflow into the hearts of others. As we've been loved, we love without qualification; as we've been forgiven, we forgive initiatively, even before people ask; as we've been blessed, we bless others with affirmation and assurance.

Gracious day to you! May all your days be filled with the Lord's fullness with grace upon grace.

LLOYD JOHN OGILVIE

FLOWER—LARKSPUR • BIRTHSTONE—RUBY

JULY

ESTHER

7, 8, 9, 10

1

ACTS

9:22-43

PSALM 18:2   **THE LORD IS MY ROCK,** and my fortress, and my deliverer; my God, my strength, in whom I will trust; my buckler, and the horn of my salvation, and my high tower.

_____

_____

_____

_____

JOB

1, 2, 3

2

ACTS

10:1-24

PSALM 148:13   Let them praise the name of the Lord: for his name alone is excellent; **HIS GLORY IS ABOVE THE EARTH AND HEAVEN.**

_____

_____

_____

_____

JOB

4, 5, 6

3

ACTS

10:25-48

PSALM 25:9   **THE MEEK WILL HE GUIDE IN JUDGMENT:** and the meek will he teach his way.

_____

_____

_____

_____

JOB

7, 8, 9

4

ACTS

11

PSALM 63:4   **THUS WILL I BLESS THEE WHILE I LIVE:** I will lift up my hands in thy name.

_____

_____

_____

_____

_____

_____

_____

_____

JULY

PSALM 16:8   **I HAVE SET THE LORD ALWAYS BEFORE ME:** because he is at my right hand, I shall not be moved.

_____
_____
_____
_____
_____

JOB
33, 34

13

ACTS
17:1-17

PSALM 3:8   **SALVATION BELONGETH UNTO THE LORD;** thy blessing is upon thy people.

_____
_____
_____
_____
_____

JOB
35, 36

14

ACTS
17:18-34

PSALM 55:14   **WE TOOK SWEET COUNSEL TO-GETHER,** and walked unto the house of God in company.

_____
_____
_____
_____
_____

JOB
37, 38

15

ACTS
18

PSALM 105:2   Sing unto him, sing psalms unto him, **TALK YE OF ALL HIS WONDROUS WORKS.**

_____
_____
_____
_____
_____

JOB
39, 40

16

ACTS
19:1-21

_____
_____
_____
_____
_____

JULY

PASS IT ON

It only takes a spark
 to get a fire going
And soon all those around
 can warm up in its glowing
That's how it is with God's love
Once you've experienced it,
 you spread His love to everyone:
You want to pass it on.

What a wondrous time is spring
 when all the trees are budding
The birds begin to sing;
 The flowers start their blooming
That's how it is with God's love
Once you've experienced it
 you want to sing
It's fresh like spring:
 You want to pass it on.

I wish for you my friend
 this happiness that I've found
You can depend on Him.
 It matters not where you're bound.
I'll shout it from the mountain top
I want my world to know:
The Lord of love has come to me.
I want to pass it on.

KURT KAISER

PASS IT ON, COPYRIGHT 1969 LEXICON MUSIC, INC.

LIFE is like an exciting book, and every year starts a new chapter.

AUTHOR UNKNOWN

THE ART OF BEING is coming into a full realization that the Master voices the secret of victorious being, when He declared that the Kingdom of God is not afar off, but that it is within you now!

WILFERD A. PETERSON

MY GARDEN

My garden is a place of prayer—
Each day I go and linger there
And oh, the joys untold I find,
The peace of heart—the peace of mind!
For as I work with His own sod
I feel much closer to my God;
Out there, beneath His clear, blue skies,
On bended knee, I raise my eyes;
Somehow, my heart is happy, free,
As there His wondrous works I see.
Each blade of grass, each flower rare
Bespeaks His love and tender care;
And as I seek His counsel fine,
Within this holy place of mine,
Again I see—in memory—
A garden called Gethsemane,
Where Jesus often went to pray
As He began another day.
I'm glad I have a garden where
I, too, can talk with God in prayer!

MADELINE G. WILSON

KEEP your face to the sunshine and you cannot see the shadow.

HELEN KELLER

THE GIFT

God gave me a friend. At once I felt within my soul the stir of nobler depths. As if with a magic wand he woke a hidden spring that rose to joyous being.

 Two souls as one became, and heart to heart we spoke in perfect unison. And thence from each went out an endless flow of love to all mankind, in thankfulness to Him who, knowing all, had drawn one to the other.

 I cry for joy! God gave me a friend!

AUTHOR UNKNOWN

JULY

SHOULD YOU GO FIRST

Should you go first and I remain
    To walk the road alone,
I'll live in memories' garden, dear,
    With happy days we've known.

In Spring I'll wait for roses red
    When fades the lilac's blue,
In early Fall when leaves turn brown
    I'll catch a glimpse of you.

Should you go first and I remain
    For battles to be fought,
Each thing you touched along the way
    Will be a hallowed spot.

I'll hear your voice, I'll see your smile
    Though blindly I may grope,
The memory of your helping hand
    Will buoy me on to hope.

Should you go first and I remain
    To finish with the scroll,
No length'ning shadows shall creep in
    To make this life seem dull.

We've known so much of happiness,
    We've had our cup of joy,
And memory is one gift of God
    That death cannot destroy.

Should you go first and I remain,
    One thing I'd have you do . . .
Walk slowly down that long lone path,
    For soon I'll follow you.

I'll want to know each step you take
    That I may walk the same,
For someday, down that lonely road . . .
    You'll hear me call your name.

ALBERT ROWSWELL

FORGIVENESS is an opportunity that Christ extended to us on the cross. When we accept His forgiveness and are willing to forgive ourselves, then we find relief.

BILLY GRAHAM

YES, LORD

Jesus, I give all of this to you. Jesus, I just started out to dream for my neighborhood. I didn't ask you to make me a messenger to the world. I just wanted to love my neighbors. But Jesus, here it is. Here's my future, here's my loneliness, here are all the pressures, here are the criticisms, and I gave Him everything. And I told Him to take me again and I would try to make "Yes, Lord" the continuing motto of my life.

ANN KIEMEL

THE WORLD is bathed in the love of God, as it is flooded by the blessed sun. If we are in the light and walk in love, our walk will be with God, and His gentleness will make us great.

HUGH BLACK

OVER THE HILLS

Over the hills and far away
    An old man lingers at close of day;
Now that his journey is almost done
    His battles fought
      and his victories won—
The old-time honesty and truth,
Trustfulness and the friends of youth,
    Home and mother—where are they?
Over the hills and far away—
    Over the hills and far away!

EUGENE FIELD

JULY

JOB
41, 42

17

ACTS
20:1-19

PSALM 33:8   LET ALL THE EARTH FEAR THE LORD: let all the inhabitants of the world stand in awe of him.

_____
_____
_____
_____
_____

PSALMS
1, 2, 3, 4

18

ACTS
20:20-41

PSALM 86:12   I will praise thee, O Lord my God, with all my heart: and I WILL GLORIFY THY NAME FOR EVERMORE.

_____
_____
_____
_____
_____

PSALMS
5, 6, 7, 8

19

ACTS
21:1-20

PSALM 20:5   WE WILL REJOICE IN THY SALVATION; and in the name of our God we will set up our banners: the Lord fulfill all thy petitions.

_____
_____
_____
_____
_____

PSALMS
9, 10, 11, 12

20

ACTS
21:21-40

PSALM 25:21   Let integrity and uprightness preserve me; FOR I WAIT ON THEE.

_____
_____
_____
_____
_____

_____
_____
_____
_____
_____

JULY

PSALM 71:23   MY LIPS SHALL GREATLY RE-JOICE when I sing unto thee; and my soul, which thou hast redeemed.

_____
_____
_____
_____
_____

PSALMS
13, 14, 15

21

ACTS
22

PSALM 22:11   BE NOT FAR FROM ME; for trouble is near; for there is none to help.

_____
_____
_____
_____
_____
_____

PSALMS
16, 17, 18

22

ACTS
23:1-17

PSALM 37:22   FOR SUCH AS BE BLESSED OF HIM SHALL INHERIT THE EARTH, and they that be cursed of him shall be cut off.

_____
_____
_____
_____
_____

PSALMS
19, 20, 21

23

ACTS
23:18-35

PSALM 138:1   I WILL PRAISE THEE WITH MY WHOLE HEART: before the gods will I sing praise unto thee.

_____
_____
_____
_____
_____
_____

PSALMS
22, 23, 24

24

ACTS
24

JULY

PSALMS
25, 26, 27, 28

25

ACTS
25

PSALM 147:3   HE HEALETH THE BROKEN IN HEART, and bindeth up their wounds.

_____
_____
_____
_____
_____

PSALMS
29, 30, 31, 32

26

ACTS
26

PSALM 72:13   HE SHALL SPARE THE POOR AND NEEDY, and shall save the souls of the needy.

_____
_____
_____
_____
_____

PSALMS
33, 34, 35, 36

27

ACTS
27:1-22

PSALM 26:2   EXAMINE ME, O LORD, and prove me; try my reins and my heart.

_____
_____
_____
_____
_____

PSALMS
37, 38, 39, 40

28

ACTS
27:23-44

PSALM 37:16   A LITTLE THAT A RIGHTEOUS MAN HATH IS BETTER than the riches of the wicked.

_____
_____
_____
_____
_____
_____
_____

JULY

PSALM 95:1   O come, let us sing unto the Lord: **LET US MAKE A JOYFUL NOISE TO THE ROCK OF OUR SALVATION.**

_____
_____
_____
_____
_____

PSALMS
41, 42, 43, 44

29

ACTS
28

PSALM 105:7   **HE IS THE LORD OUR GOD:** his judgments are in all the earth.

_____
_____
_____
_____
_____
_____

PSALMS
45, 46, 47, 48

30

ROMANS
1

PSALM 63:7   Because thou hast been my help, **THEREFORE IN THE SHADOW OF THY WINGS WILL I REJOICE.**

_____
_____
_____
_____
_____

PSALMS
49, 50, 51, 52

31

ROMANS
2

FAITH, HOPE, LOVE

Faith has been rediscovered. Hope has been rediscoverd. And now love is being rediscovered. But the greatest of these is love!

ANNE ORTLUND

_____
_____
_____
_____
_____

JULY

ACQUAINTANCES upon this earth are all you'd ever know, if trouble had always passed you by, and grief you'd never known. Time was I used to nod at the one who lived across the way. I knew her name and she knew mine. We passed the time of day; little did she mean to me and nothing I to her. Then one morning sorrow came my way and my world was grey.

I saw her face, felt her hand, and knew she'd come to lend the strength I needed. And right then I found I had a friend.

It's not in sunshine that friends are often made, but when our skies are grey. Splendid souls are seldom on display; we cannot tell what lies behind the casual nod or smile.

Remember . . . it is only when we face the cares that life must send, we realize that the casual neighbor has changed into a friend.

AUTHOR UNKNOWN

Someone like you makes the heart
    seem the lighter,
Someone like you makes the day's
    work worthwhile,
Someone like you makes the sun
     shine the brighter,
Someone like you makes a sigh
    half a smile.
Life's an odd pattern of briars
    and roses,
Clouds sometimes darken, no sun
    shining through,
Then the cloud lifts and the
     sunlight discloses
Near to me, dear to me—
    someone like you.

JAMES W. FOLEY

I CAN'T BE PERFECT and it's futile to try to be. What I do try to be is surrendered. It's not easy and I fail often—too often. But I know where to go for healing and a new slate. I don't have to be shot down to ground level again every time I sin. I can get things right with God, ask his forgiveness and strength, and pick up where I left off. The dying to self and the growing are what it's all about. It's not the trying, it's the dying.

B.J. THOMAS

YOU WILL FIND, as you look back upon your life, that the moments when you have really lived are the moments when you have done things in the spirit of love.

HENRY DRUMMOND

WE are apt to forget, amid the pressure of life's burdens, that the divine love is personal, individual, discriminating, and unchanging, and that through ways we know not, the Lord is leading us on. When we seem the most deserted, He may be drawing us nearer to Himself.

AUTHOR UNKNOWN

WHAT BETTER WAY for us to show our love and gratitude to God for His salvation gift to us, than to share the bread of our salvation with others!

AL BRYANT

ALL THINGS work together for good to those who love God. Have patience, have faith, have hope, have love as you stand at the foot of Christ's cross, and hold fast to it—the anchor of the soul and reason as well as the heart.

CHARLES KINGSLEY

JULY

A MARVELOUS WORK

What a marvelous work God has done in my life! To have come, by His grace, from a nervous, depressed, fearful, insecure, neurotic, hopeless human being to a person born of God, filled with His spirit, overflowing with the rivers of living waters, full of joy, peace, hope, patience, love, gentleness, faith, temperance, and great concern for others, is an absolute miracle of God. He very sovereignly brought me into Davidic praise and worship, which has brought me into His Presence. There the shackles and bonds that had been loosed but were still a shadow in my life are being taken away. There I am finding greater and greater liberty of faith. There I am finding my desires being conformed to His. There I am finding more and more fulfillment for all those desires, hopes and dreams each day. There I am learning to hope His hopes and dream His dreams bigger and bigger. There I have found my true love in all His splendor and grandeur, and there I shall continue to grow in all of this by His grace.

ANNE MURCHISON

August

I STAND BY THE DOOR

An Apologia for My Life

I stand by the door. I neither go too far in, nor stay too far out, the door is the most important door in the world—it is the door through which men walk when they find God.

There's no use my going way inside, and staying there, when so many are still outside and they, as much as I, crave to know where the door is. And all that so many ever find is only the wall where a door ought to be. They creep along the wall like blind men, with feeble outstretched, groping hands. Feeling for a door, knowing there must be a door, yet they never find it . . . so I stand by the door.

The most tremendous thing in the world is for men to find that door—the door to God. The most important thing any man can do is to take hold of one of those blind, groping hands, and put it on the latch—the latch that only clicks and opens to the man's own touch. Men die outside that door, as starving beggars die on cold nights in cruel cities in the dead of winter—die for want of what is within their grasp.

I admire the people who go way in. But I wish they would not forget how it was before they got in. Then they would be able to help the people who have not yet even found the door, or the people who want to run away again from God. You can go in too deeply, and stay in too long, and forget the people outside the door. As for me, I shall take my old accustomed place, near enough to God to hear Him, and know He is there, but not so far from men as not to hear them, and remember they are there, too. Where? Outside the door—thousands of them, millions of them. But—more important for me —one of them, two of them, ten of them, whose hands I am intended to put on the latch. So I shall stand by the door and wait for those who seek it.

"I had rather be a door-keeper . . ." So I stand by the door.

SAMUEL MOOR SHOEMAKER

FLOWER—POPPY • BIRTHSTONE—SARDONYX

AUGUST

PSALMS
53, 54, 55, 56

1

ROMANS
3

PSALM 104:33   **I WILL SING UNTO THE LORD AS LONG AS I LIVE:** I will sing praise to my God while I have my being.

_____
_____
_____
_____
_____

PSALMS
57, 58, 59

2

ROMANS
4

PSALM 121:7   **THE LORD SHALL PRESERVE THEE FROM ALL EVIL:** he shall preserve thy soul.

_____
_____
_____
_____
_____

PSALMS
60, 61

3

ROMANS
5

PSALM 36:11   **LET NOT THE FOOT OF PRIDE COME AGAINST ME,** and let not the hand of the wicked remove me.

_____
_____
_____
_____
_____

PSALMS
62, 63

4

ROMANS
6

PSALM 56:3   What time I am afraid, **I WILL TRUST IN THEE.**

_____
_____
_____
_____
_____
_____
_____

AUGUST

PSALM 7:10   MY DEFENCE IS OF GOD, which saveth the upright in heart.

_____
_____
_____
_____
_____
_____
_____

PSALMS
64, 65

5

ROMANS
7

PSALM 38:15   . . . FOR IN THEE, O LORD, DO I HOPE: thou wilt hear, O Lord my God.

_____
_____
_____
_____
_____
_____
_____

PSALMS
66, 67

6

ROMANS
8:1-19

PSALM 79:9   HELP US, O GOD OF OUR SALVATION, FOR THE GLORY OF THY NAME: and deliver us, and purge away our sins, for thy name's sake.

_____
_____
_____
_____
_____
_____

PSALMS
68, 69

7

ROMANS
8:20-39

PSALM 104:31   THE GLORY OF THE LORD SHALL ENDURE FOR EVER: the Lord shall rejoice in his works.

_____
_____
_____
_____
_____
_____

PSALMS
70, 71, 72

8

ROMANS
9:1-16

_____
_____
_____
_____
_____
_____

AUGUST

PSALMS
73, 74, 75

9

ROMANS
9:17-33

PSALM 119:47 . . . AND I WILL DELIGHT MYSELF IN THY COMMANDMENTS, which I have loved.

_____
_____
_____
_____
_____

PSALMS
76, 77, 78

10

ROMANS
10

PSALM 150:1 PRAISE YE THE LORD. Praise God in his sanctuary: praise him in the firmament of his power.

_____
_____
_____
_____
_____

PSALMS
79, 80

11

ROMANS
11:1-18

PSALM 31:16 MAKE THY FACE TO SHINE UPON THY SERVANT: save me for thy mercies' sake.

_____
_____
_____
_____
_____

PSALMS
81, 82, 83

12

ROMANS
11:19-36

PSALM 52:8 . . . But I am like a green olive tree in the house of God: I TRUST IN THE MERCY OF GOD FOR EVER AND EVER.

_____
_____
_____
_____
_____

_____
_____
_____
_____
_____

AUGUST

PSALM 69:30   **I WILL PRAISE THE NAME OF GOD WITH A SONG,** and will magnify him with thanksgiving.

PSALMS
84, 85

13

ROMANS
12

PSALM 18:3   **I WILL CALL UPON THE LORD,** who is worthy to be praised: so shall I be saved from mine enemies.

PSALMS
86, 87

14

ROMANS
13

PSALM 37:31   **THE LAW OF HIS GOD IS IN HIS HEART;** none of his steps shall slide.

PSALMS
88, 89

15

ROMANS
14

PSALM 91:2   I will say of the Lord, **HE IS MY REFUGE AND MY FORTRESS:** my God; in him will I trust.

PSALMS
90, 91

16

ROMANS
15:1-16

AUGUST

LORD, lift me out of the frustration of trying to decide whether I am loving with your love, and help me to get out on a limb in caring about people. I know all along you will love through me in ways beyond my strength. Amen.

LLOYD JOHN OGILVIE

THE DREAMS AHEAD

. . . Each of us has his golden goal,
    Stretching far into the years;
And ever he climbs with a hopeful soul,
    With alternate smiles and tears.
To some it's a dream of home and wife;
    To some it's a crown above;
The dreams ahead are what make each life
    The dreams—and faith—and love!

EDWIN CARLISLE LITSEY

THINK OF . . .
Stepping on shore, and finding it Heaven! Taking hold of a hand, and finding it God's! Breathing new air, and finding it celestial! Feeling invigorated, and finding it immortality! Passing from the storm to unbroken calm! Waking to life—and finding it home!

AUTHOR UNKNOWN

EVERY PROBLEM is an opportunity for God, and He is looking for committed people through whom He can work.

ANNE MURCHISON

THE LORD IS READY to love another through us anytime we are ready to let ourselves be the channel of that love. That is the whole position of Scripture. When we are ready to consent to love, he is quite ready to love.

RAY C. STEDMAN

I DO NOT WALK ALONE

Because God walked with me
    Through all my yesteryears,
I now can read the meaning
    Of all my grief and tears.
Because God walks with me
    Within this world today,
I face tough times assured
    He'll help me all the way.
Because God walks with me
    Down paths untrod, unknown,
I know no fear because
    I do not walk alone.

PERRY TANKSLEY

THE ART OF AWARENESS

It is identifying yourself with the hopes, dreams, fears and longings of others, that you may understand them and help them.

WILFERD A. PETERSON

PRAYER is a direction of life, a focusing of one's most personal and deepest attention Godward. The purpose is to love God and learn to know Him so well, that our wills, our actions will be more and more aligned with His, until even our unconscious reactions and purposes will have the mark of His love, His life about them.

KEITH MILLER

O Thou,
Whose stillness drowns
earth's total noise,
only in Thee
is stillness found . . .
And I rejoice.

RUTH BELL GRAHAM

AUGUST

THE PRAYER PERFECT

Dear Lord! Kind Lord!
    Gracious Lord! I pray
Thou wilt look on all I love,
    Tenderly today!
Weed their hearts of weariness;
    Scatter every care
Down a wake of angel-wings
    Winnowing the air.
And with all the needy
    O divide, I pray,
This vast measure of content
    That is mine today!

JAMES WHITCOMB RILEY

If I can stop one heart from breaking,
I shall not live in vain;
If I can ease one life the aching,
Or cool one pain,
Or help one fainting robin
Unto his nest again,
I shall not live in vain.

EMILY DICKINSON

HAND IN HAND

If I may walk with you, my love,
My feet shall never go astray;
This age-old promise ever new
I give you with my heart today.

No trial, then, too great to bear;
No challenge that I dare not meet . . .
As long as you are there to care,
I find my pathways all are sweet.

You are my key to happiness
In everything I strive to do.
I ask of life no more than this . . .
To walk, love, hand in hand with you.

NADINE BROTHERS LYBARGER

A good man there was, of religion,
Who was a poor parson of a town; . . .
This noble example to his sheep he gave
That first he wrought,
    and afterward he taught.
And, though he holy was and virtuous,
He was not merciless to sinful man,
Nor in his speech formidable nor proud,
But in his teaching discreet and benign.
To draw folk unto heaven
    by the beauty of a life,
        and example—this was his business.
He waited not for pomp and reverence.
Nor made sophisticated his conscience;
But the love of Christ
    and his apostles twelve,
He taught, and first
        he followed it himself.

GEOFFREY CHAUCER

HOLY STAR

O Father, may that holy star
    Grow every year more bright,
And send its glorious beams afar
    To fill the world with light.

WILLIAM CULLEN BRYANT

TO LOVE means to communicate to the other, that you will never fail him or let him down when he needs you, but that you will always be standing by with all the necessary encouragements. It is something one can communicate to another only if one has it.

ASHLEY MONTAGU

IF instead of a gem, or even a flower, we could cast the gift of a lovely thought into the heart of a friend, that would be giving as the angels give.

GEORGE McDONALD

AUGUST

PSALMS
92, 93

17

ROMANS
15:17-33

PSALM 118:8   IT IS BETTER TO TRUST IN THE LORD than to put confidence in man.

_____
_____
_____
_____
_____
_____

PSALMS
94, 95, 96

18

ROMANS
16

PSALM 142:7   BRING MY SOUL OUT OF PRISON, that I may praise thy name: the righteous shall compass me about; for thou shalt deal bountifully with me.

_____
_____
_____
_____

PSALMS
97, 98

19

1 CORINTHIANS
1

PSALM 100:1   MAKE A JOYFUL NOISE UNTO THE LORD, all ye lands.

_____
_____
_____
_____
_____
_____

PSALMS
99, 100

20

1 CORINTHIANS
2

PSALM 30:4   SING UNTO THE LORD, O ye saints of his, and give thanks at the remembrance of his holiness.

_____
_____
_____
_____
_____
_____
_____

AUGUST

PSALM 97:12   **REJOICE IN THE LORD, YE RIGHT-EOUS;** and give thanks at the remembrance of his holiness.

_____
_____
_____
_____
_____

PSALMS
101, 102, 103

21

1 CORINTHIANS
3

PSALM 27:1   **THE LORD IS MY LIGHT AND MY SALVATION;** whom shall I fear? the Lord is the strength of my life; of whom shall I be afraid?

_____
_____
_____
_____
_____

PSALMS
104, 105, 106

22

1 CORINTHIANS
4

PSALM 100:4   Enter into his gates with thanksgiving, and into his courts with praise: **BE THANKFUL UNTO HIM AND BLESS HIS NAME.**

_____
_____
_____
_____
_____

PSALMS
107, 108, 109

23

1 CORINTHIANS
5

PSALM 80:19   Turn us again, O Lord God of hosts, **CAUSE THY FACE TO SHINE; AND WE SHALL BE SAVED.**

_____
_____
_____
_____
_____

PSALMS
110, 111

24

1 CORINTHIANS
6

_____
_____
_____
_____
_____

AUGUST

PSALMS
112, 113, 114

25

1 CORINTHIANS
7:1-20

PSALM 112:3 Wealth and riches shall be in his house: and HIS RIGHTEOUSNESS ENDURETH FOR EVER.

PSALMS
115, 116, 117

26

1 CORINTHIANS
7:21-40

PSALM 16:11 Thou wilt shew me the path of life: IN THY PRESENCE IS FULNESS OF JOY; at thy right hand there are pleasures evermore.

PSALM
118

27

1 CORINTHIANS
8

PSALM 40:8 I DELIGHT TO DO THY WILL, O MY GOD: yea, thy law is within my heart.

PSALM
119:1-60

28

1 CORINTHIANS
9

PSALM 47:6 SING PRAISES TO GOD, SING PRAISES: sing praises unto our King, sing praises.

AUGUST

PSALM 118:14   THE LORD IS MY STRENGTH and song, and is become my salvation.

_____
_____
_____
_____
_____
_____

PSALM
119:61-120

29

1 CORINTHIANS
10:1-16

PSALM 42:8   Yet the Lord will command his lov-ingkindness in the daytime, and IN THE NIGHT HIS SONG SHALL BE WITH ME, and my prayer unto the God of my life.

_____
_____
_____
_____

PSALM
119:121-176

30

1 CORINTHIANS
10:17-33

PSALM 89:26   HE shall cry unto me, THOU ART MY FATHER, MY GOD, AND THE ROCK OF MY SAL-VATION.

_____
_____
_____
_____
_____

PSALMS
120, 121

31

1 CORINTHIANS
11:1-17

CHERISH EACH DAY

**Make Prayer
the key of the morning
and
the lock of the evening.**

RONALD E. GARMAN

_____
_____
_____
_____
_____
_____

AUGUST

PRAY

Pray when in the mood, it is sinful to
neglect such an opportunity. Pray when
not in the mood, it is dangerous to be
in such a condition.

Pray
when all your soul
a tiptoe stands
in wistful eagerness
to talk with God;
put out your hands,
God bends to hear;
it would be sin
not to draw near.

Pray
when gray inertia
creeps through your soul,
as though a man
who fights the cold,
then growing languid
slumbereth,
and slumbering
know not
it is death.

Pray
when swamped
with sin and shame
and nowhere else
to pin the blame
but your own will
and waywardness;
God knows you,
loves you nonetheless.

So . . .
pray.

RUTH BELL GRAHAM

❦

OH, ALL OF US, who are children of
God! How untaught we are in how to
treat each other! How distracted we are
by our lonely pursuits! How numb we
are to each other's private pain! How
totally desperate some of us are to know
and to be known—to have someone, or
just a few, who really care!

Reach anew to God, then reach to
each other. Only then can you reach out
to the world.

ANNE ORTLUND

THE NEW DIMENSION OF LOVE

I know that they live again, that they
live again, my dear ones whom I no
longer can see.

MARJORIE HOLMES

IT'S HOW YOU LIVE

It's not the church you belong to;
    It's not the gifts you give;
It's not the creed you subscribe to;
    It's how you daily live.
It's not the woes and pain you face
    Or the absence of strife,
And it's not prayers or hymns you sing;
    It's how you live your life.

It's not the faith your lips profess
    Nor grand success you win;
It's how you act toward those in need.
    It's how you live, my friend.

PERRY TANKSLEY

IF A GENEROUS SPIRIT characterizes
your home, where every member gives
rather than takes, your home will be a
reflection of heaven!

AL BRYANT

AUGUST

SACRIFICE

Every man who desires the pearl of great price must sacrifice his all to buy it. It is not enough to see the beauty and the glory and almost to taste the joy of this wonderful life; you must become the possessor of it. The man had found and seen, desired and rejoiced in the pearl of great price; but he did not have it until he gave up everything and bought it.

You cannot live every day in perfect fellowship with God without giving time to it. Hours, days, weeks, months, and years are gladly given by men and women to perfect themselves in some profession or accomplishment. Do you expect the Christian walk is so easy and cheap that without giving time you can find close fellowship with God? But this pearl is worth everything. If you find there is struggle in your heart, never mind. By God's grace, if you will lie at His feet, you may depend upon it—deliverance will come!

ANDREW MURRAY

September

I WALK WITH GOD

Reflecting God's Love to Others

Sincerity and integrity may not be the most glamorous qualities sought after by our society. Yet if it is to survive at all, if it is to be saved from ultimate decadence, if it is to be restored to some semblance of its former greatness, truth and fidelity must flourish again.

And this is possible only if these qualities first find genuine expression in the lives of God's people.

It is in this connection that I would here give great credit to the essential integrity of the character of Christ. Perhaps as a rough, rather rugged man, no other single attribute in the life of our Lord has drawn me to Him with such enormous impetus.

It is the strength of His honesty, it is the total trustworthiness of His character, it is the utter credibility of His commitments to me that have drawn and bound my wild, willful, wayward spirit to Himself with bonds of steel.

He is in truth and in fact my fondest friend. He is in living reality my most loyal companion amid a chaotic society. He is the precious person, deeply appreciated, who is ever "the perfect gentleman" because of His impeccable, unfailing conduct toward me.

God, my Father, all through a long and exciting life has never betrayed me. He has never deceived me. He has never double-crossed me. Any tiny fragment of faith and confidence ever invested in Him, He has always honored. He has made good on all His commitments to me as a common man. What greater confidence can one find today than to walk in company with such a companion?

So it is that something of that comradeship and association with God's Spirit should express itself in my spirit. It need not be stunning; it need not be sensational. But it does need to be so sincere that others will see and know that I walk with God, and He with me.

W. PHILLIP KELLER
COPYRIGHT 1981 W. PHILLIP KELLER

FLOWER—ASTER • BIRTHSTONE—SAPPHIRE

SEPTEMBER

PSALMS
122, 123, 124

1

1 CORINTHIANS
11:18-34

PSALM 9:1   I WILL PRAISE THEE, O LORD, with my whole heart; I will shew forth all thy marvellous works.

_____
_____
_____
_____
_____

PSALMS
125, 126, 127

2

1 CORINTHIANS
12

PSALM 32:5   I acknowledged my sin unto thee, and mine iniquity have I not hid. I said, I will confess my transgressions unto the Lord; AND THOU FORGAVEST THE INIQUITY OF MY SIN.

_____
_____
_____
_____

PSALMS
128, 129, 130

3

1 CORINTHIANS
13

PSALM 71:8   LET MY MOUTH BE FILLED WITH THY PRAISE and with thy honour all the day.

_____
_____
_____
_____
_____

PSALMS
131, 132, 133

4

1 CORINTHIANS
14:1-21

PSALM 50:23   WHOSO OFFERETH PRAISE GLORIFIETH ME: and to him that ordereth his conversation aright will I shew the salvation of God.

_____
_____
_____
_____
_____
_____
_____
_____

SEPTEMBER

PSALM 119:62   AT MIDNIGHT I WILL RISE TO GIVE THANKS UNTO THEE because of thy righteous judgments.

_____
_____
_____
_____
_____
_____

**PSALMS
134, 135, 136**

5

**1 CORINTHIANS
14:22-40**

PSALM 101:1   I WILL SING OF MERCY AND JUDGMENT: unto thee, O Lord, will I sing.

_____
_____
_____
_____
_____
_____

**PSALMS
137, 138, 139**

6

**1 CORINTHIANS
15:1-20**

PSALM 55:16   . . . As for me, I will call upon God; AND THE LORD SHALL SAVE ME.

_____
_____
_____
_____
_____
_____

**PSALMS
140, 141, 142**

7

**1 CORINTHIANS
15:21-40**

PSALM 96:6   Honour and majesty are before him: STRENGTH AND BEAUTY ARE IN HIS SANCTUARY.

_____
_____
_____
_____
_____
_____

**PSALMS
143, 144, 145**

8

**1 CORINTHIANS
15:41-58**

_____
_____
_____
_____
_____

SEPTEMBER

PSALMS
146, 147, 148

9

1 CORINTHIANS
16

PSALM 98:4   Make a joyful noise unto the Lord, all the earth: MAKE A LOUD NOISE, AND REJOICE, AND SING PRAISE.

_____
_____
_____
_____
_____

PSALMS
149, 150

10

2 CORINTHIANS
1

PSALM 31:3   . . . FOR THOU ART MY ROCK AND MY FORTRESS; therefore for thy name's sake lead me, and guide me.

_____
_____
_____
_____
_____

PROVERBS
1, 2, 3

11

2 CORINTHIANS
2

PSALM 46:1   GOD IS OUR REFUGE AND STRENGTH, a very present help in trouble.

_____
_____
_____
_____
_____

PROVERBS
4, 5, 6

12

2 CORINTHIANS
3

PSALM 89:52   BLESSED BE THE LORD for evermore. Amen and Amen.

_____
_____
_____
_____
_____

_____
_____
_____
_____
_____

SEPTEMBER

PSALM 33:22　　　LET THY MERCY, O LORD, BE UPON US, according as we hope in thee.

_____
_____
_____
_____
_____
_____
_____

PROVERBS
7, 8

13

2 CORINTHIANS
4

PSALM 86:1　　　BOW DOWN THINE EAR, O LORD, HEAR ME: for I am poor and needy.

_____
_____
_____
_____
_____
_____
_____

PROVERBS
9, 10

14

2 CORINTHIANS
5

PSALM 125:4　　　DO GOOD, O LORD, UNTO THOSE THAT BE GOOD, and to them that are upright in their hearts.

_____
_____
_____
_____
_____
_____

PROVERBS
11, 12

15

2 CORINTHIANS
6

PSALM 73:28　　　. . . But it is good for me to draw near to God: I HAVE PUT MY TRUST IN THE LORD GOD, that I may declare all thy works.

_____
_____
_____
_____
_____
_____
_____
_____

PROVERBS
13, 14

16

2 CORINTHIANS
7

SEPTEMBER

ECCLESIASTES 3:1-13

To every thing there is a season, and a time to every purpose under the heaven: A time to be born, and a time to die; a time to plant, and a time to pluck up that which is planted; A time to kill, and a time to heal; a time to break down, and a time to build up; A time to weep, and a time to laugh; a time to mourn, and a time to dance; A time to cast away stones, and a time to gather stones together; a time to embrace, and a time to refrain from embracing; A time to get, and a time to lose; a time to keep, and a time to cast away; A time to rend, and a time to sew; a time to keep silence, and a time to speak; A time to love, and a time to hate; a time of war, and a time of peace. What profit hath he that worketh in that wherein he laboureth? I have seen the travail, which God hath given to the sons of men to be exercised in it. He hath made every thing beautiful in his time: also he hath set the world in their heart, so that no man can find out the work that God maketh from the beginning to the end. I know that there is no good in them, but for a man to rejoice, and to do good in his life. And also that every man should eat and drink and enjoy the good of all his labour, it is the gift of God.

IT IS IN SICKNESS that we most feel the need of that sympathy which shows how much we are dependent one upon another for our comfort and even necessities. Thus disease, opening our eyes to the realities of life, is an indirect blessing.

HOSEA BALLOU

Count your garden by the flowers,
Never by the leaves that fall;
Count your days by golden hours,
Don't remember clouds at all!

Count your nights by stars, not shadows,
Count your life by smiles—not tears;
And on this and each tomorrow,
Count your age by friends—not years.

You will never grow old if you have
a goal and a purpose to achieve.
You will never grow old if you have
the power to hope and to believe.

You will always be young if you take
your place in the march of new ideas,
For you'll have the zest and the best
of youth, with the wisdom of the years.

AUTHOR UNKNOWN

I DO NOT MIND being in this wheelchair a few short years if indeed it means priceless, precious souls are going to be gathered into the family of God.

JONI EARECKSON

Just as God gives to each rose
    a gentle touch of dew,
And gives unto each evening sky
    the lovely sunset's hue,
So may He give to you this day
    from His enduring love,
Great happiness and heart's content
    and blessings from above.

AUTHOR UNKNOWN

EACH FAMILY grows out of a unique and meaning/full history . . . and each family is growing into a unique and meaning/full future.

L. RICHARD LESSOR

SEPTEMBER

INCREDIBLE as it may seem, God wants our companionship. He wants to have us close to Him. He wants to be a father to us, to shield us, to protect us, to counsel us, and to guide us in our way through life.

BILLY GRAHAM

A BIRTHDAY WISH

I do not wish you joy without a sorrow,
    Nor endless day
      without the healing dark,
Nor brilliant sun
without the restful shadow,
    Nor tides that never turn
      against your bark.

I wish you love, and strength,
and faith, and wisdom,
    Good, gold—enough
      to help some needy one.
I wish you songs,
but also blessed silence,
    And God's sweet peace
      when every day is done.

DOROTHY NELL McDONALD

THERE IS no friendship, no love, like that of the parent for the child.

HENRY WARD BEECHER

O GOD, grant to our minds that illumination without which we walk in darkness and know not whither we go. Remember us, O Lord, who do not always remember Thee, and help us to accomplish our tasks without tension or strain, that we may do good work and merit Thy blessing. For Jesus' sake. Amen.

PETER MARSHALL

Beyond the partings and the pains
    beyond the sighing and the tears,
how beautiful to be with God
    through all the endless, blessed years.

AUTHOR UNKNOWN

I LIFT THE BRANCH

As I grow older day by day
And heartaches add to wisdom's bay,
The loves for which my youth once vied
No longer light my fires, inside.
I lift the branch that's hanging low.
I smell the rose but let it grow.
Adventure lacks the lure it knew
When foolish dreams, and passions grew
And though it still demands my smile
(Where past and present meet awhile)
No more I haunt the turtle's rest
Or flush the robin from her nest.
I journey, now, to meet an end
Where deeds of past the future blend
And what I pass, in love's embrace,
I leave for better in its place—
But God must often hear me say:
I wish I lived my life this way.

MICHAEL DUBINA

GOD did not create woman from man's head, that he should command her, nor from his feet, that she should be his slave, but rather from his side, that she should be near his heart.

AUTHOR UNKNOWN

THE ART OF BEING

It is a philosophy of being today, instead of becoming in a tomorrow that never comes.

WILFERD A. PETERSON

SEPTEMBER

PROVERBS
15, 16

17

2 CORINTHIANS
8

PSALM 118:6   The Lord is on my side; I WILL NOT FEAR: what can man do unto me?

_____
_____
_____
_____
_____
_____

PROVERBS
17, 18

18

2 CORINTHIANS
9

PSALM 34:3   O magnify the Lord with me, and LET US EXALT HIS NAME TOGETHER.

_____
_____
_____
_____
_____
_____

PROVERBS
19, 20, 21

19

2 CORINTHIANS
10

PSALM 58:11   So that a man shall say, VERILY THERE IS A REWARD FOR THE RIGHTEOUS: verily he is a God that judgeth in the earth.

_____
_____
_____
_____
_____

PROVERBS
22, 23

20

2 CORINTHIANS
11:1-16

PSALM 92:1   IT IS A GOOD THING TO GIVE THANKS UNTO THE LORD, and to sing praises unto thy name, O most High . . . .

_____
_____
_____
_____
_____

_____
_____
_____
_____

SEPTEMBER

PSALM 104:19   HE APPOINTED THE MOON FOR SEASONS: the sun knoweth his going down.

_____
_____
_____
_____
_____
_____

PROVERBS
24, 25

21

2 CORINTHIANS
11:17-33

PSALM 78:1   GIVE EAR, O MY PEOPLE, TO MY LAW: incline your ears to the words of my mouth.

_____
_____
_____
_____
_____
_____

PROVERBS
26, 27

22

2 CORINTHIANS
12

PSALM 112:4   Unto the upright there ariseth light in the darkness: HE IS GRACIOUS, AND FULL OF COMPASSION, AND RIGHTEOUS.

_____
_____
_____
_____
_____

PROVERBS
28, 29

23

2 CORINTHIANS
13

PSALM 56:13   For thou has delivered my soul from death: wilt not thou deliver my feet from falling, THAT I MAY WALK BEFORE GOD IN THE LIGHT OF THE LIVING.

_____
_____
_____

PROVERBS
30, 31

24

GALATIANS
1

_____
_____
_____
_____
_____

SEPTEMBER

ECCLESIASTES
1, 2, 3, 4

25

GALATIANS
2

PSALM 119:27   **MAKE ME TO UNDERSTAND THE WAY OF THY PRECEPTS: so shall I talk of thy wondrous works.**

_____
_____
_____
_____
_____

ECCLESIASTES
5, 6, 7, 8

26

GALATIANS
3

PSALM 127:3   **LO, CHILDREN ARE AN HERITAGE OF THE LORD: and the fruit of the womb is his reward.**

_____
_____
_____
_____
_____

ECCLESIASTES
9, 10, 11, 12

27

GALATIANS
4

PSALM 29:11   **The Lord will give strength unto his people; THE LORD WILL BLESS HIS PEOPLE WITH PEACE.**

_____
_____
_____
_____
_____

SONG OF SOLOMON
1, 2, 3

28

GALATIANS
5

PSALM 34:7   **THE ANGEL OF THE LORD ENCAMPETH ROUND ABOUT THEM that fear him, and delivereth them.**

_____
_____
_____
_____
_____

_____
_____
_____
_____
_____

SEPTEMBER

PSALM 37:3   TRUST IN THE LORD, AND DO GOOD; so shalt thou dwell in the land, and verily thou shalt be fed.

_____
_____
_____
_____
_____

SONG OF SOLOMON
4, 5, 6

29

GALATIANS
6

PSALM 118:24   THIS IS THE DAY WHICH THE LORD HATH MADE; we will rejoice and be glad in it.

_____
_____
_____
_____
_____

SONG OF SOLOMON
7, 8

30

EPHESIANS
1

OUR LORD'S PRAYER

Our Father which art in heaven,
Hallowed be thy name
Thy kingdom come.
Thy will be done in earth,
as it is in heaven
Give us this day our daily bread
And forgive us our debts,
as we forgive our debtors
And lead us not into temptation,
but deliver us from evil:
For thine is the kingdom,
and the power,
and the glory,
for ever. Amen . . .

MATTHEW 6:9-13

_____
_____
_____
_____
_____

SEPTEMBER

LORD, YOU'VE GIVEN ME SO MUCH

Lord, you've given me so much
Brought me this far in a short time,
Still there's so much room to grow;
Help me to never stop,
    never stop searching
For ways I can serve You more.
When I look back through the years,
Time after time
    I would fall from you;
Yet You gently picked me up
Gave me a second chance,
Brought me back home at last
Grace so amazing to me.
The way you work through me
Is a mystery.
But help me see, how I can be
More of Your helper,
    more of Your child,
More of Your image inside.

Lord, You've given me so much
Friends and loved ones
    surround my day,
Yet in one who gave His life,
I found the perfect peace
I found a perfect expression of love
    in this world.
Help me to never stop,
    never stop searching
For ways I can serve You more.

JOHN PURIFOY

THE ART OF FRIENDSHIP

To be a friend a man should strive to lift people up, not cast them down; to encourage, not discourage; to set an example that will be an inspiration to others.

WILFERD A. PETERSON

O GOD, I acknowledge that I have sinned against You. I am sorry for my sins. I am willing to turn from my sins. I openly receive and acknowledge Jesus Christ as my Savior. I confess Him as Lord. From this moment on I want to live for Him and serve Him. In Jesus' name. Amen.

BILLY GRAHAM

TO LOVE abundantly is to live abundantly, and to love forever is to live forever.

AUTHOR UNKNOWN

A WALK IN LOVE

Who seeks for heaven alone to save his soul may keep the path, but will not reach the goal; while he who walks in love may wander far, yet God will bring him where the blessed are.

HENRY VAN DYKE

DEAR HEART

This much my spirit understands . . .
Our hearts are always holding hands.
Beside me, or my distant star,
My happiness is where you are.

Through laughter, sorrow, joy or tears,
Closer and closer through the years.
This much my spirit understands . . .
Our hearts are always holding hands.

OPAL WINSTEAD

BETWEEN THE HUMBLE and contrite heart and the majesty of heaven there are no barriers; the only password is prayer.

HOSEA BALLOU

SEPTEMBER

OPPORTUNITIES

This is the beginning of a new day. God has given this day to me to use as I will. I can waste it or use it. I can make it a day long to be remembered for its joy, its beauty and its achievement, or it can be filled with pettiness.

What I do today is important because I am exchanging a day of my life for it. When tomorrow comes, this day will be gone forever, but I shall hold something which I have traded for it. It may be no more than a memory, but if it is a worthy one I shall not regret the price. I want it to be gain not loss, good not evil, success not failure.

Here is a day, and here am I. God will not expect more of me than I am capable of giving, but I must live up to my best. There will be beauty and I must not miss it. There will be cries of people in distress, and I must hear and answer. There will be moments of temptation, but I must not yield. There will be times of tension, but I must not speak impulsively. There will be opportunties, and I must be ready.

When night comes, I want to look back without regret, and forward with radiant spirit and thankful heart.

SAMUEL F. PUGH

October

LOVING ARMS SURROUND ME

Praise for God's Peace and Comfort

When I feel the mist and chill of rain,
When I feel the loneliness of pain,
Father, how Your loving arms surround me,
Closing in with peace and warmth around me! . . .
Then I know
    You're right in all You do,
And my spirit sings,
    content in You.

When my life seems full of push and press,
Caught in agitation and distress,
Father, how Your loving arms surround me,
Closing in with peace and warmth around me! . . .
Then I rest
    in all You are, and do,
And my spirit sings,
    content in You.

When I feel the failures of my years,
Years of weakness, selfishness, and fears,
Father, how Your loving arms surround me,
Closing in with peace and warmth around me! . . .
Then I feel
    forgiven, washed, and new,
And I bow in thanks,
    and worship You.

ANNE ORTLUND
COPYRIGHT 1981 ANNE ORTLUND

FLOWER—CALENDULA • BIRTHSTONE—OPAL

OCTOBER

ISAIAH
1, 2, 3

1

EPHESIANS
2

PSALM 9:2   I WILL BE GLAD AND REJOICE IN THEE: I will sing praise to thy name.

_____
_____
_____
_____
_____
_____

ISAIAH
4, 5, 6

2

EPHESIANS
3

PSALM 116:5   Gracious is the Lord, and right-eous; yea, OUR GOD IS MERCIFUL.

_____
_____
_____
_____
_____
_____

ISAIAH
7, 8, 9

3

EPHESIANS
4

PSALM 56:12   Thy vows are upon me, O God: I WILL RENDER PRAISES UNTO THEE.

_____
_____
_____
_____
_____
_____

ISAIAH
10, 11, 12

4

EPHESIANS
5:1-17

PSALM 119:160   Thy word is true from the beginning: and EVERY ONE OF THY RIGHTEOUS JUDGMENTS ENDURETH FOR EVER.

_____
_____
_____
_____
_____
_____

OCTOBER

PSALM 78:7   That they might set their hope in God, and not forget the works of God, but KEEP HIS COMMANDMENTS . . . .

ISAIAH
13, 14, 15

5

EPHESIANS
5:18-33

PSALM 119:10   WITH MY WHOLE HEART HAVE I SOUGHT THEE: O let me not wander from thy commandments.

ISAIAH
16, 17, 18

6

EPHESIANS
6

PSALM 147:5   Great is our Lord, and of great power: HIS UNDERSTANDING IS INFINITE.

ISAIAH
19, 20, 21

7

PHILIPPIANS
1

PSALM 31:1   IN THEE, O LORD, DO I PUT MY TRUST; let me never be ashamed: deliver me in thy righteousness.

ISAIAH
22, 23, 24

8

PHILIPPIANS
2

OCTOBER

ISAIAH
25, 26, 27

9

PHILIPPIANS
3

PSALM 39:13   **O SPARE ME, THAT I MAY RECOVER STRENGTH,** before I go hence, and be no more.

_____
_____
_____
_____
_____

ISAIAH
28, 29, 30

10

PHILIPPIANS
4

PSALM 94:22   . . . But the Lord is my defence; and **MY GOD IS THE ROCK OF MY REFUGE.**

_____
_____
_____
_____
_____

ISAIAH
31, 32, 33

11

COLOSSIANS
1, 2

PSALM 119:114   **THOU ART MY HIDING PLACE** and my shield: I hope in thy word.

_____
_____
_____
_____
_____

ISAIAH
34, 35

12

COLOSSIANS
3, 4

PSALM 54:1   **SAVE ME, O GOD, BY THY NAME,** and judge me by thy strength.

_____
_____
_____
_____
_____

_____
_____
_____
_____
_____

OCTOBER

PSALM 89:14   Justice and judgment are the habitation of thy throne: MERCY AND TRUTH SHALL GO BEFORE THY FACE.

ISAIAH

36, 37

13

1 THESSALONIANS

1

PSALM 82:8   ARISE, O GOD, JUDGE THE EARTH: for thou shalt inherit all nations.

ISAIAH

38, 39, 40

14

1 THESSALONIANS

2

PSALM 107:31   OH THAT MEN WOULD PRAISE THE LORD FOR HIS GOODNESS, and for his wondrous works to the children of men.

ISAIAH

41, 42

15

1 THESSALONIANS

3

PSALM 44:18   OUR HEART IS NOT TURNED BACK, neither have our steps declined from thy way. . . .

ISAIAH

43, 44, 45

16

1 THESSALONIANS

4

OCTOBER

THE ART OF LOVE

Love is the dove of peace, the spirit of brotherhood; it is tenderness and compassion, forgiveness and tolerance.

WILFERD A. PETERSON

As we offer our small rejoicing
  For the love that surrounds our days,
All the wonderful works
      of Thy goodness
  Shall open before our gaze;
Through the gates of our narrow
      thanksgiving
  We shall enter Thy courts of praise.

ANNIE JOHNSON FLINT

WHAT IS A THANKFUL HEART?

. . . A thankful heart is one which has discovered the secret of looking beyond itself, to God, and it can experience joy in all its fullness because it has also known sorrow.

. . . A thankful heart is one which has grown out of itself and into the lives of others, and sees the good in every experience of life.

. . . A thankful heart is one which "lets not a day or night unhallowed pass, but still remembers what the Lord hath done."

AUTHOR UNKNOWN

FINDING THE BEAUTIFUL

Though we travel the world over to find the beautiful, we must carry it with us, or we find it not.

RALPH WALDO EMERSON

YOU SHOULD always be learning from those who know more than you do, and you should always be teaching those who know less. All of us are forever responsible to be son, brother, or father —daughter, sister, or mother—depending on the spiritual level of the one to whom we're relating at the moment.

ANNE ORTLUND

LORD, help me to put into words and action the way I feel about the people of my life. I pray that no one with whom I come in contact today will have to wonder how I feel about them. Amen.

LLOYD JOHN OGILVIE

SUCCESS

He has achieved success who has lived well, laughed often and loved much; who has gained the respect of intelligent men and the love of little children; who has filled his niche and accomplished his task; who has left the world better than he found it, whether by an improved poppy, a perfect poem or a rescued soul; who has never lacked appreciation of earth's beauty or failed to express it; who has looked for the best in others and given the best he had; whose life was an inspiration; whose memory is a benediction.

MRS. A. J. STANLEY

HOME

Every house where love abides and friendship is a guest, is surely home, and home, sweet home, for there the heart can rest.

HENRY VAN DYKE

OCTOBER

I HOPE you'll give yourself in measurable, fresh ways to God. What will those ways be? He longs for your time, your words, your worship, your affection. Make him happy! I want to, too. Wherever you are spiritually, give yourself afresh to God.

Then after that—in the light of that —give yourself to his beautiful family, also waiting to be loved. They're all around you. They're lonely. They're hungry to know the Bible and grow; to be given time, to be patted and hugged and laughed with and cried with and counseled. They, too, want you, yourself! Nothing less will do.

And, oh, my friend, isn't it amazing that some day Jesus will even say, "Truly I say to you, to the extent that you did it to one of these brothers of mine, even the least of them, you did it to me . . . ?

"You loved the members of my family—you loved me. For them you inconvenienced yourself; you went without, to complete their material needs; you entered into my sufferings in order to fill them full; for them you endured hassle and strain—and your greatest joy was their maturity and completion. You shared my goals for them!

"Thank you! Well done! Enter into your rewards (did you dream they would be this wonderful?)! You make me so happy. Don't you understand now why, on my part, the cross was worth it all? Even the least saint is so precious!

"Let me give you another hug. You loved my family—you loved me. It wasn't easy; I know. I watched you every moment, and I interceded for you, that you would persevere . . . . And you did! I'm filled with exceeding joy. You identified with my sufferings; you were willing! Oh, my dear one!

"Come. We've both suffered; now let's go celebrate together."

ANNE ORTLUND

NOTHING is more highly to be prized than the value of each day.

JOHANN WOLFGANG VON GOETHE

OUR LIVES are a manifestation of what we think about God.

AUTHOR UNKNOWN

GOD ASKS NO MAN whether he will accept life. That is not the choice. You must take it. The only choice is how.

HENRY WARD BEECHER

A BOND OF BROTHERHOOD

God employs His people to encourage one another. We should be glad that God usually works for man by man. It forms a bond of brotherhood, and being mutually dependent on one another, we are fused more completely into one family. Fellow Christians, take the text as God's message to you. Aim to comfort the sorrowful, and to cheer the despondent. Speak a word in season to him who is weary, and encourage those who are fearful to go on their way with gladness. God encourages you by His promises; Christ encourages you as He points to the heaven He has won for you, and the Spirit encourages you as He works in you to will and to do of His own will and pleasure.

CHARLES H. SPURGEON

OCTOBER

ISAIAH
46, 47, 48

17

1 THESSALONIANS
5

PSALM 118:23   **THIS IS THE LORD'S DOING;** it is marvellous in our eyes.

_____
_____
_____
_____
_____
_____

ISAIAH
49, 50, 51

18

2 THESSALONIANS
1

PSALM 74:17   **THOU HAST SET ALL THE BORDERS OF THE EARTH:** thou hast made summer and winter.

_____
_____
_____
_____
_____
_____

ISAIAH
52, 53, 54

19

2 THESSALONIANS
2

PSALM 117:1   **O PRAISE THE LORD, ALL YE NATIONS;** praise him, all ye people.

_____
_____
_____
_____
_____

ISAIAH
55, 56, 57

20

2 THESSALONIANS
3

PSALM 62:12   **ALSO UNTO THEE, O LORD, BELONGETH MERCY:** for thou renderest to every man according to his work.

_____
_____
_____
_____
_____
_____
_____

OCTOBER

PSALM 5:7 . . . But as for me, I will come into thy house in the multitude of thy mercy: AND IN THY FEAR WILL I WORSHIP TOWARD THY HOLY TEMPLE.

ISAIAH
58, 59, 60

21

1 TIMOTHY
1, 2

PSALM 25:14 THE SECRET OF THE LORD IS WITH THEM THAT FEAR HIM: and he will shew them his covenant.

ISAIAH
61, 62, 63

22

1 TIMOTHY
3

PSALM 9:8 AND HE SHALL JUDGE THE WORLD in righteousness, he shall minister judgment to the people in uprightness.

ISAIAH
64, 65, 66

23

1 TIMOTHY
4

PSALM 34:5 THEY LOOKED UNTO HIM, AND WERE LIGHTENED: and their faces were not ashamed.

JEREMIAH
1, 2, 3

24

1 TIMOTHY
5

OCTOBER

JEREMIAH
4, 5, 6

25

1 TIMOTHY
6

PSALM 10:12   Arise, O Lord; O God, lift up thine hand: **FORGET NOT THE HUMBLE.**

___

JEREMIAH
7, 8, 9

26

2 TIMOTHY
1

PSALM 59:9   Because of his strength will I wait upon thee: **FOR GOD IS MY DEFENCE.**

___

JEREMIAH
10, 11, 12

27

2 TIMOTHY
2

PSALM 26:1   Judge me, O Lord; for I have walked in mine integrity; **I HAVE TRUSTED ALSO IN THE LORD;** therefore I shall not slide.

___

JEREMIAH
13, 14, 15

28

2 TIMOTHY
3, 4

PSALM 121:8   **THE LORD SHALL PRESERVE THY GOING OUT AND THY COMING IN** from this time forth, and even for evermore.

OCTOBER

PSALM 119:103   HOW SWEET ARE THY WORDS UNTO MY TASTE! yea, sweeter than honey to my mouth!

_____
_____
_____
_____
_____

JEREMIAH
16, 17, 18

29

TITUS
1

PSALM 63:3   Because thy lovingkindness is better than life, MY LIPS SHALL PRAISE THEE.

_____
_____
_____
_____
_____

JEREMIAH
19, 20, 21

30

TITUS
2

PSALM 56:10   In God will I praise his word: IN THE LORD WILL I PRAISE HIS WORD.

_____
_____
_____
_____
_____

JEREMIAH
22, 23, 24

31

TITUS
3

WE SHALL LOVE EACH OTHER BETTER

In the great Home-coming and Reunion of hearts, all the veils which obscure feeling will be torn down, and we shall know each other better, and shall love each other better.

AUTHOR UNKNOWN

_____
_____
_____
_____
_____

OCTOBER

THOSE WHO LIVE with an active attitude of kindness, compassion, mercy, and concern for all of life are essentially persons of great inner light. There is a radiance and effulgence of enthusiasm and well-being about them. Warmth, affection, and good cheer emanate from them. It is the life and love of God apparent. This kindness dispels darkness, lifts loads, speaks peace, and inspires the downhearted.

W. PHILLIP KELLER

COMPENSATION

There is no loss,
    however great the seeming;
There is no power
    to keep the soul from gain;
For life and love,
    however dim the dreaming
Must end sometime in peace,
    all free from pain.
Each life must sometime
    know this great unveiling;
Must sometime gather
    up the harvest sown—
Roses will bloom
    through seasons never failing . . .
The heart rejoice
    and grief be overthrown.

AUTHOR UNKNOWN

. . . GOD CONVERSES with me through ordinary circumstances, things, places, and people I encounter. It's when I'm most in need of that daily breath from God that he sends me a pure whiff of spiritual oxygen in the most practical way—through something in my everyday world!

JEANNE HILL

THE EXTRAORDINARY THINGS about kindness is that the more you expend, the richer you become. Try it. Do a little quiet thinking about people around you. Make an effort to understand them better; then take the trouble to speak words that may lift their spirit, enhance their self-respect. You can never guess what a few kind words sincerely spoken may do for them—and for you.

THE LITTLE GAZETTE

I WALKED AWAY from that couple knowing more than ever before that to really love, to make "Yes, Lord" the motto of your life or mine, is to be vulnerable. It's to allow Jesus to take out or put in whatever he wants.

ANN KIEMEL

UNTIL that glorious day—"Till Armageddon"—let us live for Christ. Let us trust Him. Let us turn to Him in our time of need. And let us joyfully walk hand in hand with our Lord Jesus Christ —regardless of our circumstances—until we personally and physically join Him throughout eternity!

BILLY GRAHAM

HAPPINESS is a perfume you cannot pour on others without getting a few drops on yourself.

AUTHOR UNKNOWN

OUR LORD, our God, deliver us from the fear of what might happen and give us the grace to enjoy what now is and to keep striving after what ought to be. Through Jesus Christ our Lord. Amen.

PETER MARSHALL

OCTOBER

A PSALM

Thank God for love.
For mother's love,
  deep as the valley of shadows;
For father's love,
  high as the mountains;
For brother's love,
  constant as breathing;
For sister's love,
  cleansing as sunlight;
For children's love,
  searching as conscience;
For friendship's love,
  bracing as trials;
For lover's love,
  strong as eternity—
  Thank God for love.

ELINOR LENNEN

November

A GIFT OF THE HEART

Living in a Faith Relationship

The greatest recurring problem that I have encountered as a minister working with people is that many folks do not know how to have faith. They do not know where to get faith, they do not know how to give faith—you know they'd give it if they could get it, but they don't know where to find it.

The word in Christian faith is not intellectual, the word is union. How can you get in union with God? Follow these steps:

1. <u>SEED OF FAITH:</u> The desire in your heart to have a governed relationship with Jesus.
2. <u>ROOT OF FAITH:</u> The confession that you are inadequate and unworthy for the relationship with Jesus.
3. <u>GROWTH OF FAITH:</u> The experience of new growth in your relationship with Jesus as you repent, remove and remodel your life and personality.
4. <u>BUD OF FAITH:</u> The personal persistence in the heartfelt desire to confess, repent, remove and remodel your life.
5. <u>FLOWER OF FAITH:</u> The fragrance comes when GOD is ready for you to have the fun, fellowship, and joy with Jesus that will enrich your relationship with Him.

Number 4, the bud is when you must persist in all of the things in 1, 2 and 3. You've got to persist and if you don't persist in these things and sustain them, then where are you? You have revealed you did not want a governed relationship with Christ in the first place. Persistence is the mark of integrity.

Heavenly Father, some people have a difficult time because they don't know how to relate to other people, much less to You. Relationships tend to be one-way streets. We expect people to invest in us and give of themselves, but we just don't give back and don't invest in our relationships. Lord, before we begin to talk to You about having faith, we ask that You'll help us to begin to have faith in one another. If we can't live in a faith relationship with those brothers and sisters whom we have seen, we will never be able to live in a relationship with You whom we have not yet seen and must receive in faith. Work through us, Lord, in the progression of readiness to receive Your gift of the heart.

REVEREND RICHARD M. FREEMAN

FLOWER—CHRYSANTHEMUM • BIRTHSTONE—TOPAZ

NOVEMBER

PSALM 74:21   O let not the oppressed return ashamed: LET THE POOR AND NEEDY PRAISE THY NAME.

PSALM 120:1   IN MY DISTRESS I CRIED UNTO THE LORD, and he heard me.

PSALM 6:2   HAVE MERCY UPON ME, O LORD; for I am weak; O Lord, heal me; for my bones are vexed.

PSALM 93:2   Thy throne is established of old: THOU ART FROM EVERLASTING.

NOVEMBER

PSALM 33:12   **BLESSED IS THE NATION WHOSE GOD IS THE LORD; and the people whom he hath chosen for his own inheritance.**

_____
_____
_____
_____
_____

JEREMIAH
34, 35

5

HEBREWS
5

PSALM 62:6   **HE ONLY IS MY ROCK AND MY SALVATION: he is my defence; I shall not be moved.**

_____
_____
_____
_____
_____

JEREMIAH
36, 37

6

HEBREWS
6

PSALM 132:8   **ARISE, O LORD, INTO THY REST; thou, and the ark of thy strength.**

_____
_____
_____
_____
_____
_____

JEREMIAH
38, 39

7

HEBREWS
7:1-14

PSALM 99:9   **EXALT THE LORD OUR GOD, and worship at his holy hill; for the Lord our God is holy.**

_____
_____
_____
_____
_____
_____

JEREMIAH
40, 41

8

HEBREWS
7:15-28

_____
_____
_____
_____
_____

NOVEMBER

JEREMIAH
42, 43, 44

9

HEBREWS
8

PSALM 34:13   KEEP THY TONGUE FROM EVIL, and thy lips from speaking guile.

_____
_____
_____
_____
_____
_____
_____

JEREMIAH
45, 46

10

HEBREWS
9:1-14

PSALM 97:6   THE HEAVENS DECLARE HIS RIGHTEOUSNESS, and all the people see his glory.

_____
_____
_____
_____
_____
_____

JEREMIAH
47, 48

11

HEBREWS
9:15-28

PSALM 122:9   Because of the house of the Lord our God **I WILL SEEK THY GOOD.**

_____
_____
_____
_____
_____
_____

JEREMIAH
49, 50

12

HEBREWS
10:1-19

PSALM 67:1   GOD BE MERCIFUL UNTO US, and bless us; and cause his face to shine upon us.

_____
_____
_____
_____
_____
_____
_____
_____
_____

NOVEMBER

PSALM 17:5   **HOLD UP MY GOINGS IN THY PATHS,** that my footsteps slip not.

_____
_____
_____
_____
_____
_____

LAMENTATIONS
1, 2

13

HEBREWS
10:20-39

PSALM 47:7   **FOR GOD IS THE KING OF ALL THE EARTH:** sing ye praises with understanding.

_____
_____
_____
_____
_____
_____

LAMENTATIONS
3, 4, 5

14

HEBREWS
11:1-20

PSALM 66:2   **SING FORTH THE HONOUR OF HIS NAME:** make his praise glorious.

_____
_____
_____
_____
_____
_____

EZEKIEL
1, 2, 3

15

HEBREWS
11:21-40

PSALM 25:10   **ALL THE PATHS OF THE LORD ARE MERCY AND TRUTH** unto such as keep his covenant and his testimonies.

_____
_____
_____
_____
_____
_____
_____
_____

EZEKIEL
4, 5, 6

16

HEBREWS
12

NOVEMBER

ETERNAL LOVE

I have loved you dearly as a sweetheart and will continue to love you as my wife. But over and above that, I love you with a Christian love that demands that I never react in any way toward you that would jeopardize our prospects of entering heaven, which is the supreme objective of both our lives. And I pray that God Himself will make our affection for one another perfect and eternal.

JAMES C. DOBSON, SR.

JOY

Confess your sin, receive Jesus as your Savior—and then begin a new life with Him. You will find God's peace in your heart, His guidance in your life, and the comfort of His presence through your suffering—through your personal armageddon, whatever form it may take.

BILLY GRAHAM

LOVE

Sunshine and love go hand in hand,
Scatter them everywhere.
The more you give unselfishly,
Much more will be yours to share.
Living in deeds of sunshine and love,
Smiles thrown in for good measure,
Will cause the darkest clouds to depart,
Filling your day with pleasure.
Those who wish to give of themselves
Need have no thought of fine gold—

For he who giveth and loveth much,
Hath built up wealth untold.

EDNA GARLAND HALL

I AM THANKFUL

With each Thanksgiving Day I pause in the solitude of my own meditation to thank God for the unseen bounties which surround me every day of my life.

With each Thanksgiving Day I am thankful for the blessings of family and friends who have enriched my life.

With each Thanksgiving Day I am thankful for the spiritual assurances which sustain my faith and act as a lamp to my feet through a world of doubt.

With each Thanksgiving Day I am thankful for the harvest, for the gold grain and the ripened fruit, for the mysterious affinity which puts the color in the plants and the fragrance in the flowers.

With each Thanksgiving Day I am thankful for the birds which sing their lullabies at eventide and welcome the morning with their glorious oratorios.

With each Thanksgiving Day I am thankful for the light which reveals the beauties of creation and the darkness which reflects the glories of God in the heavens.

Why, bless your hearts, each Thanksgiving Day I'm thankful to be alive!

C. F. SKIRVIN

Thanksgiving is an attitude,
A never failing gratitude,
That fills my bosom all the year,
And makes each hour a bit more dear.

MILDRED ALBERT

NOVEMBER

THE LOVE OF GOD is an event! The love of God is a person! The love of God is Jesus Christ! We experience God's love because Jesus Christ, the living Lord, made it possible for us to have a vital, personal relationship with God.

EARL F. PALMER

Let Autumn be our teacher;
Everything must sleep and die,
To rise and live again.

JOHN E. VANCE

THERE ARE three requisites to the proper enjoyment of earthly blessings: a thankful reflection on the goodness of the giver; a deep sense of our own unworthiness; and a recollection of the uncertainty of our long possessing them. The first will make us grateful, the second humble, and the third moderate.

HANNAH MORE

EACH MOMENT of the year has its own beauty, a picture which was never seen before and which shall never be seen again.

RALPH WALDO EMERSON

PRAISE AND WORSHIP will not only open up your relationship with God. It will enable you to express yourself and your love to others more readily, and it will open up a greater sense of enjoyment in all things as well. We all need to love and to be loved.

ANNE MURCHISON

TROUBLE AND PERPLEXITY drive me to prayer, and prayer drives away perplexity and trouble.

PHILIP MELANCHTHON

THANKSGIVING is a rich harvest of the heart after the fruit and grain are stored away, the quiet season of remembering, the moment when we pause to praise and pray.

AUTHOR UNKNOWN

THE ART OF MARRIAGE

A good marriage must be created. In the
    art of marriage the little things
    are the big things . . .

It is never being too old to hold hands.

It is remembering to say, "I love you,"
    at least once each day.

It is never going to sleep angry.
It is forming a circle of love that
    gathers in the whole family.

It is speaking words of appreciation
    and demonstrating gratitude
    in thoughtful ways.

It is having the capacity to forgive
    and forget.

It is finding room for the things
    of the spirit.

It is not only marrying the right partner,
It is being the right partner.

WILFERD A. PETERSON

FOR SPIRITUAL BLESSINGS, let our prayers be importunate, perpetual and persevering; for temporal blessings, let them be general, short, conditional and modest.

JEREMY TAYLOR

NOVEMBER

EZEKIEL
7, 8

17

HEBREWS
13

PSALM 37:30   THE MOUTH OF THE RIGHTEOUS SPEAKETH WISDOM, and his tongue talketh of judgment.

EZEKIEL
9, 10

18

JAMES
1

PSALM 112:7   He shall not be afraid of evil tidings: HIS HEART IS FIXED, TRUSTING IN THE LORD.

EZEKIEL
11, 12

19

JAMES
2

PSALM 105:45   That they might observe his statutes, and keep his laws. PRAISE YE THE LORD.

EZEKIEL
13, 14

20

JAMES
3

PSALM 150:2   PRAISE HIM FOR HIS MIGHTY ACTS: praise him according to his excellent greatness.

NOVEMBER

PSALM 45:17   I WILL MAKE THY NAME TO BE REMEMBERED IN ALL GENERATIONS: therefore shall the people praise thee for ever and ever.

_____
_____
_____
_____
_____

EZEKIEL
15, 16, 17

21

JAMES
4

PSALM 28:6   BLESSED BE THE LORD, because he hath heard the voice of my supplications.

_____
_____
_____
_____
_____
_____

EZEKIEL
18, 19

22

JAMES
5

PSALM 11:7   FOR THE RIGHTEOUS LORD LOV-ETH RIGHTEOUSNESS: his countenance doth behold the upright.

_____
_____
_____
_____
_____

EZEKIEL
20, 21, 22

23

1 PETER
1

PSALM 44:26   Arise for our help, AND REDEEM US FOR THY MERCIES' SAKE.

_____
_____
_____
_____
_____

EZEKIEL
23, 24, 25

24

1 PETER
2

_____
_____
_____
_____
_____

NOVEMBER

EZEKIEL
26, 27, 28

25

1 PETER
3

PSALM 72:8 **HE SHALL HAVE DOMINION ALSO FROM SEA TO SEA,** and from the river unto the ends of the earth.

_____
_____
_____
_____
_____
_____

EZEKIEL
29, 30, 31

26

1 PETER
4

PSALM 7:11 **GOD JUDGETH THE RIGHTEOUS,** and God is angry with the wicked every day.

_____
_____
_____
_____
_____
_____

EZEKIEL
32, 33

27

1 PETER
5

PSALM 18:49 Therefore will I give thanks unto thee, O Lord, among the heathen, **AND SING PRAISES UNTO THY NAME.**

_____
_____
_____
_____
_____
_____

EZEKIEL
34, 35

28

2 PETER
1

PSALM 85:7 Shew us thy mercy, O Lord, and **GRANT US THY SALVATION.**

_____
_____
_____
_____
_____
_____
_____
_____
_____
_____

NOVEMBER

PSALM 45:6 **THY THRONE, O GOD, IS FOR EVER AND EVER: the sceptre of thy kingdom is a right sceptre.**

EZEKIEL
36, 37

29

2 PETER
2

_____
_____
_____
_____
_____

PSALM 119:89 **Forever, O Lord, THY WORD IS SETTLED IN HEAVEN.**

EZEKIEL
38, 39

30

2 PETER
3

_____
_____
_____
_____
_____

SEEK THE GOOD

Do we take the blessing that the common days bring to us? Do we extract the honey from every flower that grows by our path? Should we not learn to see the goodness and the beauty in the gifts God sends us? Their very commonness veils their blessedness. Let us seek for the good in everything. Then, though we see it not, let us never doubt that it lies hidden in every gift of God to us. Every moment brings some benediction. Even the rough hand of trial holds in its clasp for us some treasure of love.

J. R. MILLER

_____
_____
_____
_____
_____

NOVEMBER

THANKSGIVING IS NOT A DAY

Thanksgiving is not a day, it is a way of life. It is the cool of the evening and the pink and blue-purple of the sunset after a hot, bright day of traveling. It is coming home after a journey and sitting in pleasant, familiar surroundings. It is lying down after a day of labor.

Thanksgiving is gathering with your friends. It is people—old friends—between whose eyes there passes understanding; and new people whom the circle broadens to include.

Thanksgiving is modern medicine and the skilled hands of the physician. It is a brisk nurse in starchy white. It is a bouquet of flowers on the night stand and the softened eyes of those you love who gather round when you have been hurt.

Thanksgiving is the kitchen table spread with a checkered cloth. It is the aroma of ham and bean soup, and corn bread. It is a couple of wiggly children bowing their heads to say, "God is great."

Thanksgiving is the bench or the desk at which you labor. It is the family gathering in person and in memory at twilight time.

Thanksgiving is not a day, it is a way of life.

RAY L. NIXON

GOD'S SWEET DEWS and showers of grace slide off the mountains of pride and fall on the low valleys of humble hearts and make them pleasant and fertile.

AUTHOR UNKNOWN

❧

These are the amber days of
    autumn loveliness,
like people who have mellowed
    with the years and whose days hold
garnered richness of wisdom
    and remembering.

ESTHER BALDWIN YORK

A SPECIAL BIRTHDAY PRAYER

A SPECIAL BIRTHDAY PRAYER COPYRIGHT GIBSON GREETING CARDS, INC.

Thank You, God, for everything
    I've experienced here on earth—
      Thank You for protecting me
      From the moment of my birth—
And thank You for the beauty
    Around me everywhere,
The gentle rain and glistening dew,
      The sunshine and the air—
      The joyous gift of "Feeling"
The soul's soft, whispering voice
That speaks to me from deep within
    And makes my heart rejoice—
      Oh, God, no words
    are great enough
      To thank You for Just Living,
And that is why Each Birthday
Is a day for Real Thanksgiving.

HELEN STEINER RICE

THE HIGHEST REWARD for man's toil is not what he gets for it, but rather what he becomes by it.

AUTHOR UNKNOWN

WITH A GOOD CONSCIENCE our only sure reward, with history the final judge of our deeds, let us go forth to lead the land we love, asking His blessing and His help, but knowing that here on earth God's work must truly be our own.

JOHN F. KENNEDY

NOVEMBER

FATHER, WE THANK THEE

Father, we thank Thee for good health, for warm clothes to wear, for friends whose words of encouragement have often chased away dark clouds, for the zest of living, for many an answered prayer.

We thank Thee that still we live in a land bountifully able to supply all our needs, a land with peaceful valleys and smiling meadows still serene.

O help us to appreciate all that we have, to be content with it, to be grateful for it, to be proud of it.

In Thy name, to whose bounty we owe these blessings, to Thee we give our gratitude. Amen.

PETER MARSHALL

December

HE'S EVERYTHING TO ME

The Wonder of God's Grace

In the stars
　　His handiwork I see,
On the wind
　　He speaks with majesty,
Though He ruleth
　　over land and sea,

What is that to me?

I will celebrate Nativity,
　　for it has a place
in history,
Sure, He came
　　to set His people free,

What is that to me?

Till by faith
　　I met Him face to face,
and I felt the wonder
　　of His grace,

Then I knew
　　that He was more
than just a God
　　who didn't care,
that lived
　　a way out there
And now He walks
　　beside me day by day,
Ever watching o'er me
　　lest I stray,
Helping me
　　to find that narrow way,

He's ev'rything to me.
　　He's ev'rything to me.

RALPH CARMICHAEL
COPYRIGHT 1964 LEXICON MUSIC INCORPORATED

FLOWER—POINSETTIA • BIRTHSTONE—TURQUOISE

DECEMBER

EZEKIEL
40, 41, 42

1

1 JOHN
1

PSALM 144:15   Happy is that people, that is in such a case: yea, HAPPY IS THAT PEOPLE, WHOSE GOD IS THE LORD.

_____
_____
_____
_____
_____

EZEKIEL
43, 44

2

1 JOHN
2

PSALM 8:9   O Lord our Lord, HOW EXCELLENT IS THY NAME IN ALL THE EARTH!

_____
_____
_____
_____
_____

EZEKIEL
45, 46

3

1 JOHN
3

PSALM 52:9   I WILL PRAISE THEE FOR EVER, because thou hast done it: and I will wait on thy name; for it is good before thy saints.

_____
_____
_____
_____
_____

EZEKIEL
47, 48

4

1 JOHN
4

PSALM 33:21   . . . OUR HEART SHALL REJOICE IN HIM, because we have trusted in his holy name.

_____
_____
_____
_____
_____

_____
_____
_____
_____
_____

DECEMBER

PSALM 59:16 . . . But I will sing of thy power; yea, I WILL SING ALOUD OF THY MERCY IN THE MORNING: for thou hast been my defence and refuge in the day of my trouble.

DANIEL
1, 2, 3

5

1 JOHN
5

PSALM 119:2 BLESSED ARE THEY THAT KEEP HIS TESTIMONIES, and that seek him with the whole heart.

DANIEL
4, 5, 6

6

2 JOHN

PSALM 26:3 For thy loving kindness is before mine eyes: AND I HAVE WALKED IN THY TRUTH.

DANIEL
7, 8, 9

7

3 JOHN

PSALM 57:9 I WILL PRAISE THEE, O LORD, AMONG THE PEOPLE: I will sing unto thee among the nations.

DANIEL
10, 11, 12

8

JUDE

DECEMBER

HOSEA
1, 2, 3

9

REVELATION
1

PSALM 62:1   Truly my soul waiteth upon God: FROM HIM COMETH MY SALVATION.

_____
_____
_____
_____
_____
_____

HOSEA
4, 5

10

REVELATION
2:1-14

PSALM 135:13   THY NAME, O LORD, ENDUR-ETH FOR EVER; and thy memorial, O Lord, through-out all generations.

_____
_____
_____
_____
_____

HOSEA
6, 7, 8

11

REVELATION
2:15-29

PSALM 5:12   FOR THOU, LORD, WILT BLESS THE RIGHTEOUS; with favour wilt thou compass him as with a shield.

_____
_____
_____
_____
_____

HOSEA
9, 10, 11

12

REVELATION
3

PSALM 21:13   BE THOU EXALTED, LORD, in thine own strength: so will we sing and praise thy power.

_____
_____
_____
_____
_____

_____
_____
_____
_____
_____

DECEMBER

PSALM 34:8   O taste and see that the Lord is good: BLESSED IS THE MAN THAT TRUSTETH IN HIM.

HOSEA

12, 13, 14

13

REVELATION

4

PSALM 145:21   MY MOUTH SHALL SPEAK THE PRAISE OF THE LORD: and let all flesh bless his holy name for ever and ever.

JOEL

1, 2, 3

14

REVELATION

5

PSALM 24:7   Lift up your heads, O ye gates; and be ye lift up, ye everlasting doors; AND THE KING OF GLORY SHALL COME IN.

AMOS

1, 2

15

REVELATION

6

PSALM 50:14   OFFER UNTO GOD THANKSGIVING; and pay thy vows unto the most High . . . .

AMOS

3, 4, 5

16

REVELATION

7

DECEMBER

HOME FOR CHRISTMAS

May your heart be home for Christmas,
  Home where its belongings are;
Home with lights in every window,
  And the welcome-gate ajar.

Home with cherished memories dusted,
  Silver dreams all polished bright,
Bells of hope hung high for ringing,
  And faith shining in the night.

Home with laughter bubbling over
  And with kindness spread to share;
Sweet surprises in gay wrappings,
  And contentment purring there.

Home with love as its companion,
  Warm together by the fire.
May your heart be home for Christmas—
  To receive your heart's desire.

BETTY SCOTT

Christmas is sharing;
    it adds and multiplies
    as we divide it with others.

A. NIELSEN

The door is on the latch tonight,
  The heart-fire is aglow,
I seem to hear soft passing feet—
  The Christ Child in the snow.

My heart is open wide tonight
  For stranger, kith, or kin.
I would not bar a single door
  Where love might enter in.

KATE DOUGLAS WIGGIN

THE WORD OF GOD hidden in the heart is a stubborn voice to suppress.

BILLY GRAHAM

THE BIRTH OF CHRIST   Luke 2:1-40

And it came to pass in those days, that there went out a decree from Caesar Augustus, that all the world should be taxed. (And this taxing was first made when Cyrenius was governor of Syria.) And all went to be taxed, every one into his own city. And Joseph also went up from Galilee, out of the city of Nazareth, into Judaea, unto the city of David, which is called Bethlehem; (because he was of the house and lineage of David:) To be taxed with Mary his espoused wife, being great with child. And so it was, that, while they were there, the days were accomplished that she should be delivered. And she brought forth her firstborn son, and wrapped him in swaddling clothes, and laid him in a manger; because there was no room for them in the inn. And there were in the same country shepherds abiding in the field, keeping watch over their flock by night. And, lo, the angel of the Lord came upon them, and the glory of the Lord shone round about them: and they were sore afraid. And the angel said unto them, Fear not: for, behold, I bring you good tidings of great joy, which shall be to all people. For unto you is born this day in the city of David a Saviour, which is Christ the Lord. And this shall be a sign unto you; Ye shall find the babe wrapped in swaddling clothes, lying in a manger. And suddenly there was with the angel a multitude of the heavenly host praising God, saying, Glory to God in the highest and on earth peace, good will toward men. And it came to pass, as the angels were gone away from them into heaven, the

DECEMBER

shepherds said one to another. Let us now go even unto Bethlehem, and see this thing which is come to pass, which the Lord hath made known unto us. And they came with haste, and found Mary, and Joseph, and the babe lying in a manger. And when they had seen it, they made known abroad the saying which was told them concerning this child. And all they that heard it wondered at those things which were told them by the shepherds. But Mary kept all these things, and pondered them in her heart. And the shepherds returned, glorifying and praising God for all the things that they had heard and seen, as it was told unto them. And when eight days were accomplished for the circumcising of the child, his name was called JESUS, which was so named of the angel before he was conceived in the womb. And when the days of her purification according to the law of Moses were accomplished, they brought him to Jerusalem, to present him to the Lord; As it is written in the law of the Lord, Every male that openeth the womb shall be called holy to the Lord; And to offer a sacrifice according to that which is said in the law of the Lord, A pair of turtledoves, or two young pigeons. And, behold, there was a man in Jerusalem, whose name was Simeon; and the same man was just and devout, waiting for the consolation of Israel: and the Holy Ghost was upon him. And it was revealed unto him by the Holy Ghost, that he should not see death, before he had seen the Lord's Christ. And he came by the Spirit into the temple: and when the parents brought in the child Jesus, to do for him after the custom of the law, Then took he him up in his arms, and blessed God, and said, Lord, now lettest thou thy servant depart in peace, according to thy word: For mine eyes have seen thy salvation, Which thou hast prepared before the face of all people; A light to lighten the Gentiles, and the glory of thy people Israel. And Joseph and his mother marvelled at those things which were spoken of him. And Simeon blessed them, and said unto Mary his mother, Behold, this child is set for the fall and rising of many in Israel; and for a sign which shall be spoken against; (Yes, a sword shall pierce through thy own soul also,) that the thoughts of many hearts may be revealed. And there was one Anna, a prophetess, the daughter of Phanuel, of the tribe of Aser: she was of a great age, and had lived with an husband seven years from her virginity; And she was a widow of about fourscore and four years, which departed not from the temple, but served God with fastings and prayers night and day. And she coming in that instant gave thanks likewise unto the Lord, and spake of him to all them that looked for redemption in Jerusalem. And when they had performed all things according to the law of the Lord, they returned into Galilee, to their own city Nazareth. And the child grew, and waxed strong in spirit, filled with wisdom: and the grace of God was upon him. ❧

GOD'S EYES look down upon sin in judgment, but those same eyes are upon His children to bless, guide, and protect them!

AL BRYANT

DECEMBER

AMOS
6, 7, 8, 9

17

REVELATION
8

PSALM 111:1   Praise ye the Lord. I WILL PRAISE THE LORD WITH MY WHOLE HEART, in the assembly of the upright, and in the congregation.

_____
_____
_____
_____
_____

OBADIAH

18

REVELATION
9

PSALM 61:3   . . . FOR THOU HAST BEEN A SHELTER FOR ME, and a strong tower from the enemy.

_____
_____
_____
_____
_____

JONAH
1, 2, 3, 4

19

REVELATION
10

PSALM 134:2   Lift up your hands in the sanctuary, and BLESS THE LORD.

_____
_____
_____
_____
_____

MICAH
1, 2

20

REVELATION
11

PSALM 9:10   And they that know thy name will put their trust in thee: FOR THOU, LORD, HAST NOT FORSAKEN THEM THAT SEEK THEE.

_____
_____
_____
_____
_____

_____
_____
_____
_____
_____

DECEMBER

PSALM 31:14 . . . But I trusted in thee, O Lord: I said, THOU ART MY GOD.

_____
_____
_____
_____
_____
_____

MICAH
3, 4, 5

21

REVELATION
12

PSALM 24:10 Who is this King of glory? THE LORD OF HOSTS, HE IS THE KING OF GLORY.

_____
_____
_____
_____
_____
_____

MICAH
6, 7

22

REVELATION
13

PSALM 114:7 TREMBLE, THOU EARTH, AT THE PRESENCE OF THE LORD, at the presence of the God of Jacob.

_____
_____
_____
_____
_____

NAHUM
1, 2, 3

23

REVELATION
14

PSALM 33:20 Our soul waiteth for the Lord: HE IS OUR HELP AND OUR SHIELD.

_____
_____
_____
_____
_____

HABAKKUK
1, 2, 3

24

REVELATION
15

_____
_____
_____
_____
_____

DECEMBER

ZEPHANIAH
1, 2, 3

25

REVELATION
16

PSALM 86:9 **ALL NATIONS WHOM THOU HAST MADE SHALL COME AND WORSHIP BEFORE THEE, O LORD; and shall glorify thy name.**

_____
_____
_____
_____
_____

HAGGAI
1, 2

26

REVELATION
17

PSALM 72:11 **Yea, all kings shall fall down before him: ALL NATIONS SHALL SERVE HIM.**

_____
_____
_____
_____
_____

ZECHARIAH
1, 2, 3

27

REVELATION
18

PSALM 138:5 **Yea, they shall sing in the ways of the Lord: for GREAT IS THE GLORY OF THE LORD.**

_____
_____
_____
_____
_____

ZECHARIAH
4, 5, 6, 7

28

REVELATION
19

PSALM 41:13 **BLESSED BE THE LORD GOD of Israel from everlasting, and to everlasting. Amen, and Amen.**

_____
_____
_____
_____
_____

_____
_____
_____
_____
_____

DECEMBER

PSALM 68:32   Sing unto God, ye kingdoms of the earth: O SING PRAISES UNTO THE LORD . . . .

_____
_____
_____
_____
_____
_____

ZECHARIAH
8, 9, 10, 11

29

REVELATION
20

PSALM 109:30   I will greatly praise the Lord with my mouth; yea, I WILL PRAISE HIM AMONG THE MULTITUDE.

_____
_____
_____
_____
_____
_____

ZECHARIAH
12, 13, 14

30

REVELATION
21

PSALM 72:19   . . . And blessed be his glorious name for ever: and LET THE WHOLE EARTH BE FILLED WITH HIS GLORY; Amen and Amen.

_____
_____
_____
_____
_____
_____

MALACHI
1, 2, 3, 4

31

REVELATION
22

ACCEPTANCE

Acceptance always comes
before understanding.
Acceptance is faith.
ROBERT SCHULLER

_____
_____
_____
_____
_____
_____
_____

DECEMBER

ALL THESE THINGS

Christmas is holly and mistletoe
And sparkling snowy weather,
It is the old sweet carols sung,
Gay secrets we plan together.

Small stockings,
Dim in the hearthlog's glow,
Hanging expectantly;
A hovering angel, a silver star,
At the top of the fragrant tree.

Christmas is all these things
And more
It is loving and sharing and giving;
The heart within, where Christ is born,
Awakened to glorious living.

NAN HOUSTON

LOOK TO THIS DAY

Look to this day,
For it is life,
The very life of life.
In its brief course lies all
The realities and verities
            of existence,
The bliss of growth,
The Splendor of action,
The glory of power—

For yesterday is but a dream
And tomorrow is only a vision.
But today, well lived,
Makes every yesterday
            a dream of happiness
And every tomorrow
            a vision of hope.

Look well, therefore, to this day.

SANSKRIT PROVERB

HOW CAN YOU make this the happiest Christmas of your life? Simply by trying to give yourself to others. Put something of yourself into everything you give. A gift, great or small, speaks its own language. And when it tells of the love of the giver, it is truly blessed.

NORMAN VINCENT PEALE

A DEEP PRAYER LIFE with, and accountability to, some close members of the spiritual family can help make your relationship with your physical family what it ought to be.

ANNE ORTLUND

This is the wonder of Christmas—
That it brings with each passing year
A rebirth of love and of friendship,
The spirit of goodwill and cheer.

That it purges away the harshness,
The callousness, hate, and lust,
And hearts are transformed by its magic
To hearts full of faith, hope, and trust.

This is the wonder of Christmas—
That its beauty never grows dim,
And over the centuries souls are led
By the light of the Star to Him.

HELEN LOWRIE MARSHALL

THE MOTHER TO HER DAUGHTER

Then far away down the years thou shalt remember me; as when one ascends a mountain the opposite mountain lifts itself higher and higher, so as thou goest farther from me I will grow upon thee clearer and closer even than now.

EDWARD CARPENTER

DECEMBER

A CHRISTMAS WISH

May you, wherever you are in this golden hour, know joy.

May your hearthfire be surrounded with those near and dear to you.

May the happiness of your children re-echo the gladness Heaven sent forth in the time of the Miracle of Bethlehem.

May the faith the humble shepherds found in the starlit stable be yours in fullest measure.

May the exultation of Mary and Joseph light your heart with the glow of Divine love.

May you gather together in a bright bouquet love, charity, and tranquility of spirit, for he who possesses these holds the key to riches beyond measure.

May all your dreams in this splendid hour reach fulfillment.

And may all the paths you walk be lighted with peace, not only today, but in all the days of the year to come.

AUTHOR UNKNOWN

CHRISTMAS MEMORIES

CHRISTMAS IS ALL AROUND

Christmas is changing our town;
  Changing our streets, up and down
And bells ring out all around,
  All around and bells ring out
    All around.

In the contoured sands of the mind,
  Three Wise Men coming, we find
And peace settles in all around,
  All around and peace settles in
    All around.

In the center of all of our joy,
  We picture the Holiest Boy
And children play all around
  All around and children play
    All around.

We laugh at our holiday schemes;
  We sing and recount all our dreams
And we all share love all around
  All around and we all share love
    All around.

JOHN E. VANCE

Treasured Memories

LOVE IS REMEMBERING . . .

Love is remembering:
To love the Lord, our God, with all our heart, with all our soul, with all our mind, with all our strength;
To love our self;
To love our neighbor as our self;
To owe no one anything but love.

Love is remembering:
To condemn no one, to keep no score of wrong, to take no delight in the short-comings or mistakes of others, to bear no grudges.

Love is remembering:
To be patient, kind, generous, resilient;
To be receptive to the highest and best in all.

Love is remembering:
To set others free, to give them living, growing space—not to be possessive or jealous.

Love is remembering:
Not to boast, not to be conceited, not to be rude or thoughtless.

Love is remembering:
To give as we would receive, to forgive as we would be forgiven, to bless as we would be blessed, to free as we would be freed.

Love is remembering:
To love our enemies, to overcome evil with good, to pray for those who would spitefully use us, to work gently with the fearful, the ignorant, the angry elements in ourselves and others.

Love is remembering:
To let our light shine, not only when our world seems to be peaceful, harmonious, and in tune but also when it may appear warlike, inharmonious, and out of tune. Love is not dependent on outer appearances for its operation. In fair weather and in foul it shines, like the sun, on the deserving and the undeserving; it sends its healing balm on the just and the unjust, it shares its treasures with the beautiful and the unbeautiful, the weak and the strong, the lovable and the unlovable.

Love is remembering:
To believe that there is no limit to love's endurance, no end to its trust, no fading of its hope. Love can outlast anything; love never fails.

Love is remembering:
To realize that love is the best way of all, that without it all other gifts are "a noisy gong or a clanging cymbal." Without love all work, sacrifice, knowledge are meaningless.

Love is remembering:
To have faith that though now we perceive reality mostly "through a glass, darkly," a glass distorted by fear and false beliefs, the time is inevitably coming when we are finished with childish views and we will see reality as it is. And when we see reality as it truly is, we see that it is love.

Love is remembering:
To let all things be made new in love, and to give ourselves permission to become new creatures of love and life.

Treasured Memories

Love is remembering:
To give thanks that it is our Creator's good pleasure to give us the kingdom of love, life, forgiveness, freedom, and that it is our good pleasure to accept the kingdom and share it with our world.

Love is remembering:
To remember that God is love, that in our Creator there is no darkness, condemnation, nor punishment, and that we are extensions of infinite love.

Love is remembering:
To let go of fear, resentment, and guilt as they come into awareness, either through quiet contemplation or when they are triggered by the actions or in-actions of others. Perfect love casts out fear, resentment, guilt.

Love is remembering:
To remember that our neighbor is also an extension of infinite love, that we are created to be sons and daughters of our Creator, who is love, as we share this beautiful spaceship, Earth.

Love is remembering:
To know these things about love, but to know also that to be blessed we are not only to think about them in the lofty reaches of mind but to do them in the daily, down-to-earth relationships and activities of this very practical world where we live. Love is rooted in heaven but it must be lived in the earth. Practice proves love's power and reality. Love is nothing until it is shared in living.

Love is remembering:
To see yourself as a son or daughter of God and to treat yourself like one, not theoretically but practically, to treat yourself with respect, affection, appreciation, even admiration in the events of your twenty-four hour day—at breakfast, lunch, and dinner, waking, sleeping, walking, listening, talking, living, thinking, feeling. After all, you are the handiwork of God, awakening to and unfolding your divine potential.

Love is remembering:
To see others in your life as sons and daughters of God and to treat them as such, not just in moments of deep insight but especially in the tug and pull of everyday, ordinary, and extra-ordinary exchange of thought, feeling, and action. After all, they, too, are the handiwork of God, awakening to and unfolding their divine potential.

Love is remembering:
To encourage and support the unfoldment of the divine potential in yourself and in others, to enjoy and to be grateful for every relationship with awakening sons and daughters of God.

Love is remembering:
To be true to the true nature of our self which is love, to remember who we are, what we are, why we are, and where we are going.

Love is remembering:
To remember that love is our God;
Life is our religion;
Humanity is our church;
Loving our neighbor and our self
Is our daily worship.

J. SIG PAULSON

TREASURED MEMORIES

Treasured Memories

BIRTHS

A MOTHER'S LOVE

A Mother's love is something
      that no one can explain,
It is made of deep devotion
      and of sacrifice and pain,
It is endless and unselfish
      and enduring come what may
For nothing can destroy it
      or take that love away . . .
It is patient and forgiving
      when all others are forsaking,
And it never fails or falters
      even though
         the heart is breaking . . .
It believes beyond believing
      when the world around condemns,
And it glows with all the beauty
      of the rarest, brightest gems . . .
It is far beyond defining,
      it defies all explanation,
And it still remains a secret
      like the mysteries of creation . . .
A many-splendored miracle
      man cannot understand
And another wondrous evidence
      of God's tender guiding hand.

HELEN STEINER RICE

TREASURED MEMORIES

WEDDINGS

A WEDDING PRAYER

It is our earnest prayer, *not* that God shall have a part in their lives, but that He shall have the preeminent part; not that they shall possess faith, but that faith shall fully possess them both; that in a materialistic world they shall not live for the earthly and temporal alone, but that they shall be enabled to lay hold on that which is spiritual and eternal.

Let their lives together be like the course of the sun: rising in strength, going forth in power and shining more and more unto the perfect day. Let the end of their lives resemble the setting of the sun: going down in a sea of glory, only to shine on undimmed in the firmament of a better world than this.

JAMES C. DOBSON, SR.

ANNIVERSARIES

THIS IS OUR ANNIVERSARY

This anniversary day
My world seems filled with splendor,
For thoughts I think of you
        Are very, very tender.
Such gladness of this day
A special gladness borrows
When I think of the life
    We'll share through our tomorrows.
For friendship's rich reward
I'm more and more convinced
Will bring to us through life
      A richer recompense.
And if the times ahead
Are good as passing days,
Then you and I together
May face them unafraid
For love we've shared, I know,
If God bestows His mercies
Will ever deeper grow
    Through all our anniversaries.

PERRY TANKSLEY

TRADITIONAL ANNIVERSARY GIFTS

FIRST—PAPER	NINTH—WILLOW	TWENTY-FIFTH—SILVER
SECOND—COTTON	TENTH—TIN	THIRTIETH—PEARL
THIRD—LEATHER	ELEVENTH—STEEL	THIRTY-FIFTH—CORAL
FOURTH—FRUIT, FLOWERS	TWELFTH—SILK, LINEN	FORTIETH—RUBY
FIFTH—WOOD, BOOKS	THIRTEENTH—LACE	FORTY-FIFTH—SAPPHIRE
SIXTH—CANDY, IRON	FOURTEENTH—IVORY	FIFTIETH—GOLD
SEVENTH—WOOL	FIFTEENTH—CRYSTAL	SIXTIETH—DIAMOND
EIGHTH—POTTERY	TWENTIETH—CHINA	SEVENTY-FIFTH—DIAMOND

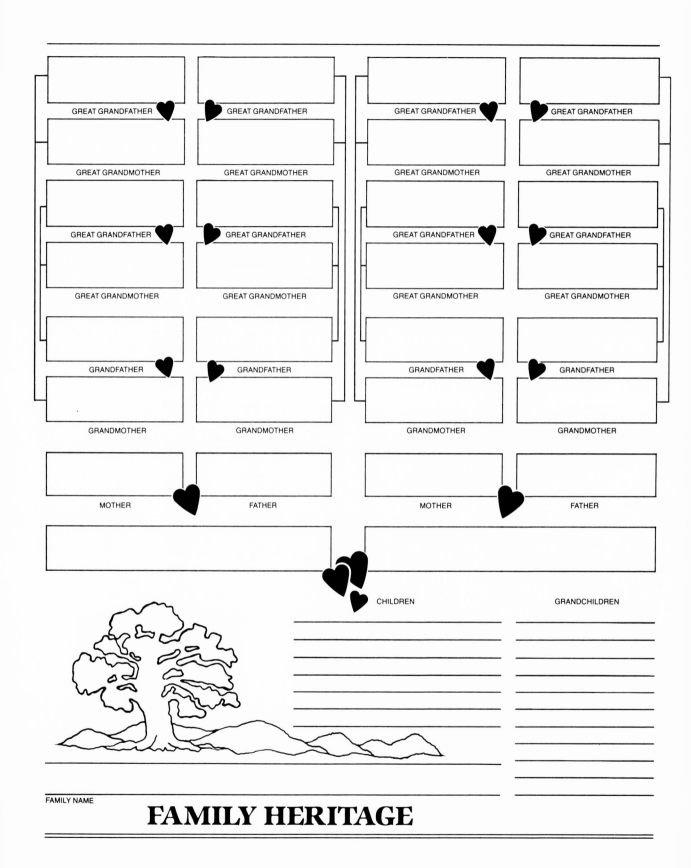

GREAT GRANDFATHER

GREAT GRANDFATHER

GREAT GRANDMOTHER

GREAT GRANDMOTHER

GREAT GRANDFATHER

GREAT GRANDFATHER

GREAT GRANDMOTHER

GREAT GRANDMOTHER

GREAT GRANDFATHER

GREAT GRANDFATHER

GREAT GRANDMOTHER

GREAT GRANDMOTHER

GREAT GRANDFATHER

GREAT GRANDFATHER

GREAT GRANDMOTHER

GREAT GRANDMOTHER

GRANDFATHER

GRANDFATHER

GRANDMOTHER

GRANDMOTHER

GRANDFATHER

GRANDFATHER

GRANDMOTHER

GRANDMOTHER

MOTHER

FATHER

MOTHER

FATHER

CHILDREN

GRANDCHILDREN

FAMILY NAME

FAMILY HERITAGE

FAMILY MEMORIES

SPECIAL BIRTHDAYS

PRECIOUS GEMS

Each birthday's like a precious gem
    That brings its beauty rare;
A treasured jewel that makes you feel
    like you're a millionaire.

The years are like bright emeralds,
    The months are rubies red,
The weeks are like a string of pearls
    Strung on a silver thread.

The days are sometimes sapphire clear,
    Or bright as opals fair,
And now and then there comes a day
    That's like a diamond rare.

The hours are like a chain of gold,
    Each link a vital part,
Binding these priceless jewels into
    A treasure for the heart.

So may the years that come to you
    Such happiness contain
That all the moments, days, and years
    Become a jeweled chain.

AUTHOR UNKNOWN

Treasured Memories

TREASURED MEMORIES

_____   _____
_____   _____
_____   _____
_____   _____
_____   _____
_____   _____
_____   _____
_____   _____
_____   _____
_____   _____
_____   _____
_____   _____
_____   _____
_____   _____
_____   _____
_____   _____
_____   _____
_____   _____
_____   _____
_____   _____
_____   _____
_____   _____
_____   _____
_____   _____
_____   _____
_____   _____
_____   _____
_____   _____
_____   _____
_____   _____

LOVED ONES WITH JESUS

SOMETIME WE'LL UNDERSTAND

Not now, but in the coming years,
It may be in the Better Land,
We'll read the meaning of our tears,
And there, sometime, we'll understand.

We'll catch the broken threads again,
And finish what we here began;
Heav'n will the mysteries explain,
And then, and then, we'll understand.

We'll know why clouds instead of sun
Were over many a cherished plan;
Why song has ceased, when scarce begun;
'Tis there, sometime, we'll understand.

Why what we long for most of all
Eludes so oft our eager hand;
Why hopes are crushed and castles fall,
Up there, sometime, we'll understand.

God knows the way, He holds the key,
He guides us with unerring Hand;
Sometime with tearless eyes we'll see;
Yes, there, up there, we'll understand.

Then trust in God through all thy days;
Fear not, for He doth hold thy hand;
Though dark thy way, still sing and praise,
Sometime, sometime, we'll understand.

MAXWELL N. CORNELIUS

CONFESSIONS

LAST DAY OF THE YEAR

Dear heavenly Father, it is the end of another year, and I raise my voice this day in praise and thanksgiving unto Thee for the many happy experiences I have enjoyed this past year. I thank Thee also for Thy guidance in overcoming the numerous trials, problems, and troubles.

Looking back, O God, I see so many things I should have done and did not, and so many words of comfort I should have uttered but was unable to find the right words to express. For all my shortcomings, which are many, I ask Thy forgiveness. Help me to realize, my God, that there will come a last day, a last opportunity, and a last prayer. So teach me to number my days, that I may apply my heart unto wisdom.

As I evaluate the year just passed, I realize that there have been many wasted days and hours; help me to make good use of every day in this coming year. In the name of Jesus I pray. Amen.

LOUISE MILLER NOVOTNY

ON THE THRESHOLD OF A NEW YEAR

Our Father, grant that in the days of this new year we may feel Thy love, the love that surrounds us, the love that will not let us go but will ever bring us back—back to Thy side, back to Thy will, back to Thy way.

We seek now Thy forgiveness, for our stupidity and our obstinacy, for the blindness of our hearts, for the wrong choices that grieved Thee and subtracted from our own happiness.

Wilt Thou forgive us, Father?

Humbly and gratefully we open our hearts to receive that great miracle of grace. We thank Thee for the fresh, strong wind of Thy Spirit which comes to bring us refreshment, cleansing, and perfect peace. Amen.

PETER MARSHALL

ONLY THE LOVE OF GOD ENDURES

Everything in life is passing
   and whatever we possess
Cannot endure forever
   but ends in nothingness,
For there are no safety boxes
   nor vaults that can contain
The possessions we collected
   and desire to retain . . .
So all that man acquires,
   Be it power, fame or jewels,
Is but limited and earthly,
   only "treasure made for fools" . . .

For only in God's Kingdom
   can man find enduring treasure,
Priceless gifts of love and beauty—
   more than mortal man can measure,
And the "riches" he accumulates,
   he can keep and part with never,
For only in God's Kingdom
   do our treasures last Forever . . .
So use the word "Forever"
   with sanctity and love,
For Nothing Is Forever
   But The Love of God Above!

HELEN STEINER RICE

BENEDICTION

May the Lord bless you and keep you,
may the Lord make his face
to shine upon you
and be gracious unto you,
and may God grant unto you His peace
in your going out
and your coming in,
in your lying down
and in your rising up,
in your labor
and in your leisure,
in your laughter
and in your tears,
until you come
to stand before Jesus
in that day in which there is no sunset
and no dawning. Amen.

ROBERT SCHULLER